THE WRITER'S WAY

THE WRITER'S WAY

Realize your creative potential and
become a successful author

SARA MAITLAND

Capella

This edition published in 2005 by Arcturus Publishing Limited
26/27 Bickels Yard, 151–153 Bermondsey Street,
London SE1 3HA

ISBN 1-84193-342-2

Printed in China

Contents

Introduction

You have opened this book and started reading it. I do not know why. I cannot know why – though I would like to say thank you.

It does not really matter whether *I* know why you are reading it, but it does matter that *you* should think a little bit about why you are reading it, or at least thinking about reading it.

Of course there are some possible reasons that are not very relevant to what happens next. Perhaps you are standing around in a bookshop waiting while your friend chooses a present for an aged aunt – and this happens to be the nearest book. Perhaps you are marooned on a desert island where, by chance, this book is the only one around. Perhaps you are just checking that the book is completely useless before you tear it up to light a fire. Perhaps you have been given the book by a totally mad relative, though in that case you might want to ask yourself why the mad relative chose to give you this book – insanity is often marked by acute perception: is there some method in the madness?

However, I am going to assume that you have picked up the book because somewhere, some part of you really wants to write – or because someone who knows you reasonably well believes that you really want to write and has given the book to you.

The first thing you may want to know is who I am and why I am writing this book. The words 'author' and 'authority', when you look at them, are obviously linked together in their meanings, and I could just say that I am the author of this book and that is my 'licence' or 'authority' but I still think you should like to know a little about the someone who is proposing to teach you something this important. This is not simply a textbook or a compilation of facts, it is an invitation to set out on an endeavour that has emotional as well as practical meaning: I'm sure you'll agree that you should not really accept an invitation from someone you know nothing about.

I have to guess which questions you want answered, but basically I was born in 1950 and grew up in London and south west Scotland. I went to Oxford University in 1968 and did a BA in English Language and Literature. I had always wanted to be a writer and in 1974 my first short stories were published in an anthology of new writers. In 1978 my first novel, *Daughter of Jerusalem*, won the Somerset Maugham Award – a well-known annual UK prize for young writers. Since then, using the opportunities that gave me, I have been a writer. I have published five more novels and five collections of short stories, but I have also branched out and written several non-fiction books, on various topics from the history of gardening to theology. I have written two radio plays and a number of other projects for the BBC. I was the last writer to work with Stanley Kubrick on his *AI* project, which is now a film of the same name directed by Stephen Spielberg; and I have written widely for magazines and anthologies. The point about all this is that I have worked with an unusually wide range of different sorts of writing.

Over the last ten or so years I have also taught creative writing to an improbable mixture of writers, ranging from prisoners to MA students, in a wide variety of ways: one-to-one mentoring, short residential courses, one-off work-shops, classes, groups and increasingly by distance learning, deploying the new technologies like email. During the 1970s I was a member of a very successful (in the sense that all the five members of the group went on to become professional writers) writers' group, which I believe enabled me to finally become a 'writer'. I started teaching in the absolute belief that we can help each other develop both our talent and our attitude and understanding of the job and this conviction has never really left me.

In the light of that I have sought out jobs where I can think about what writing means and some of the ways people might go about it.

...an endeavour that has emotional as well as practical meaning

I worked as the Literature Programmer for The Midlands Arts Centre, where I arranged events and courses in the context of an inner city arts centre, and where of course I met people doing the same thing with other forms of art. Later I became the Course Leader in Creative Writing for The Open College of the Arts, which offers accredited courses by post. From there in 2003 I became part of a project called Crossing Borders, a really exciting initiative of the British Council and Lancaster University, where we deliver mentoring courses to new African writers in nine different African countries. I tutor on this course myself but I also co-ordinate, choose and facilitate the other mentors, so I have regular contact with lots of creative writing teachers, all of whom are writers themselves, and have the chance to discuss the ways we work and share our experiences.

Meanwhile I am also teaching on the Lancaster University distance learning MA, which is delivered through email and the Internet. I am a critical reader for The Literary Consultancy and a one-to-one mentor to writers chosen by The Arts Council for England regional offices in the North East, which means that I get to work with and help writers who are further along the writing way.

All this has meant that I have an extended opportunity to think about the whole business of 'teaching' creative writing. I began to feel that I would like to pull together some of this experience, and in particular look at the odd way in which creative writing is *both* an important part of many people's identity – from their work they draw not just self-expression but also an inner sense of satisfaction and integrity – *and* a craft, which needs training, honing and working on. That is how I came to write this book and I hope it will offer a balance of these two perspectives.

In addition there is something else I want this book to do. I want it to excite you about language itself, the basic tool of our trade. This interest goes back beyond my own writing career, to my student days and even before. I believe we have to love language before we can use it fully for self-expression and communication. For me language is not just vocabulary – it is grammar and syntax and punctuation and etymology (the history of words) and a number of other things that too many people think are rather boring. For those of you who have forgotten or never learned about how mysterious and wonderful grammar itself is, I hope that this book will inspire you. To help those of you who find the whole subject either a turn off or something that makes them feel incompetent or afraid I have written a short appendix on p.232 which will explain the terms I use: just turn to it at any point if you find yourself uncertain about any technical detail of what I say.

Obviously a great deal of my thinking comes directly or indirectly from other people, and I would like to thank all my students, each of whom has probably taught me as much as I have taught them; all the other writers I have worked with and talked to over more than a quarter of a century; and especially Dr. Graham Mort, now of Lancaster University, who taught me more about creative writing and its teaching, especially within the area of new technology and distance learning, than I can begin to acknowledge. There is a great cloud of witnesses hovering within these pages.

For those of you who like to know more about the context in which someone works, I have two children, one of whom is an actress in New York and the other is studying photography in Liverpool. I now live alone joyfully in south west Scotland, and have a very rural lifestyle with a great deal of silence built into it. This is one of the best things for me about email and the opportunities it gives me both to teach and to be solitary; writing this book is an extension of that

we have to love language before we can use it fully for self-expression and communication

pleasure. At the moment I am working on a non-fiction book about silence and solitude and writing, and preparing some more short stories.

But that is enough about me. What about you?

I am going to assume that you are not yet very experienced as a writer. This really is a 'beginner's book'. There are lots of books for people who have already set out on the writer's way and feel the need for more guidance or nourishment on the journey: I have listed some of the ones that I have found useful on my own adventures in the bibliography at the end of this book. I hope you will want to try some of them when you have finished with this one.

You know you want to write creatively, and you know you want to write so that other people will want to read what you have written. However you are not sure how to go about it at any of the three levels that matter at this point:

- ❖ the emotional level
- ❖ the practical level
- ❖ the technical level

Or, to put this another way – you are not sure how to manage yourself as someone who is writing; how to manage the time and space and daily business of writing; and how to manage the writing itself. I hope that this book will help you with all three of these levels, and indeed they are quite closely related to each other. They are not really three totally separate things. I have been a professional writer for over a quarter of a century now and I am still continually moving from one level to another. I lose confidence in my ability to write, or I find I am mismanaging my writing time, or I am confronted with a new technical writing challenge that I cannot resolve – and too often it feels as though all three are happening at the same time. They are just three different ways of looking at the problem.

Why do you want to write?

You know you want to write, but before you set off on this frequently arduous and sometimes tedious journey it is worth pausing to think about *why* you want to write. There are lots of reasons why people want to write and some of them are better than others. Two of the best reasons are:

❖ You have something important to say, or a story that has to be told – but you know you do not have the writing skills to communicate it as well as it deserves or needs.

❖ You just really want to. You feel an urgent need to express something of yourself in language that goes beyond even the best conversation. This 'something' is too important to be expressed badly or clumsily.

However, some of the other reasons that people come up with are rather less good:

❖ You want to get rich. Despite anything you may read or hear, writing is a very bad way to get rich. Although there are some novelists who write international bestsellers, get fabulous sums of money for film rights and even become millionaires – they are in a tiny minority; they usually did not plan on it; and they still have to work very hard indeed. A few gamblers also become very rich, but most don't and there is always a large element of luck involved. In fact very few professional writers can survive on their genuinely creative writing alone: that is why they are always taking teaching posts, reviewing, working on community projects and doing all sorts of part-time work to subsidize their writing.

If it is hard for novelists it is even worse for other writers – no one gets rich being a poet. If you want to get rich get a proper job – one that at the very least comes with some security and a pension.

❖ You think it looks easy. If this is your main reason for starting, you should probably forget the whole thing. Good writing, as most of the best writers down all the ages will freely acknowledge, is not easy. It is both hard and hard work.

❖ You want to be a writer. This is a very different matter – lots of people want to be writers but do not really want to do the writing. They like the glamorous idea of being an artist and having an artistic, liberated, exotic lifestyle. They relish the thought of being famous or having a claim to immortality. They like the thought of jet setting around the world and attending chic literary parties, getting important phone calls from their agent and having their picture in the papers.

None of these things have anything much to do with writing, which is mostly a solitary and very unglamorous activity. Most serious writers will tell you that these sorts of things, although often good fun in themselves and well earned, are actually distractions from writing. In any case, before you can be a writer you have to do some good writing.

Of course, none of us is a hundred per cent pure-hearted. We have mixed motives even in areas like this. A fairly large dollop of ambition, or even greed, will sharpen your mind and pencil admirably; will help you through the slow difficult slog that is part of the business. An eye to what readers might like is part of the business of communicating. An awareness of what publishers might buy is particularly useful for keeping oneself focussed, especially in the later stages of self-editing, finishing and submitting one's writing. There is no excitement in the world quite like getting the first finished, printed, bound copy of your own book with your own name on it – not just your first book either: it is a delight which continues and grows with each subsequent publication.

Having said that though, I also know that it is simply an 'excitement' – it cannot compare with the deep joy and sense of power and accomplishment and fulfilment that I get when the writing itself is going well. If it were not for this sense of doing well what I most want to do, it would not be worth it.

So think about it. If you commit yourself to writing – rather than merely thinking about writing or imagining yourself writing – you are committing yourself to a great deal of frustration and hard work; to disciplined training like a marathon runner; to an activity that will inevitably cut into your spare time and irritate your friends and family; to almost inevitable disappointments (whether you are successful or whether you aren't); and to endless criticism (looked for or not), misunderstanding and straightforward rudeness from people who have, of course, never tried to do it themselves but are nonetheless the real experts because they are readers, critics or reviewers.

An eye to what readers might like is part of the business of communicating

Exercise 1 Do I really want to write?

☞ Put this book down and do something else for a while. Something that leaves your mind reasonably free – like taking a brisk walk.

☞ Think about why you bought the book and whether or not you really do want to try and write creatively. Remember that you **do not have to**. No one has to write. There is no moral or legal code that requires you, or anyone else, to write.

And that is the end of the negative section. If you are still reading, I shall assume that you really do want to write – and that you want to reach the end of this book able to write more to your own satisfaction than you feel capable of now. From here onwards, although I shall try and look at some of the reasons why writing is hard and doesn't go smoothly and feels hopeless and you want to quit and you hate language and yourself and your favourite brand of coffee, I shall not question your motivation or your desire.

Why are you reading this book?

You are a person who wants to write, and you have picked up this book because you hope it will help you achieve this. In itself this is quite curious because we are all aware that lots and lots of books, including many of the greatest works of literature and some of the most popular, long-lasting stories and poems were written by people who did not read this book – or any other book on the subject.

They did not go to creative writing workshops, or evening classes, or weekend courses. They did not study the craft of creative writing at school or university – they certainly did not get a degree in it. In a few cases, at least, when they wrote their first books, some now famous writers did not know any other writers or talk to any experts.

They wrote under difficult circumstances – scribbling away without typewriters, word processors or even decent lighting, often at the end of long days of exhausting work. This is interesting because, although there are exceptions, this is not true of creative people using other art forms.

Painters expect to study; until the nineteenth century most of them went through long and demanding apprenticeships, and since then they have still expected to study their craft and build up their skills over a long period of time. (The word 'studio' originally meant the place where the artist *studies*.) In a similar way musicians – composers as much as performers – all have teachers, and look for formal training and years of hard graft and technical learning. Even Mozart, that infant prodigy, was formally taught by his father – no one thought that even that level of talent was 'enough'. This is simply not true for writers. History, as well as the biographies of many of our contemporaries, proves that you do not necessarily need to study creative writing formally. Indeed there are lots of people who still believe that it cannot be taught.

The moral of this is that obviously you do not really need this book.

But you are reading it. There are a number of reasons why you might be reading it.

One of them is simply to save yourself time: this is a very proper motive I think. I am one of the writers who never did any formal creative writing training – although, as I've mentioned, I was in a truly wonderful, nourishing writers' group in my twenties, which was certainly a major learning experience for me. But I know, from the actual business of writing; from working with some really excellent editors; from teaching creative writing; and from sharing all these experiences with other writers, that I could have saved myself a great deal of time, energy and grief if I had known then what I have learned the hard way since.

I hope that quite a lot of this book will be about just that: about the things I wish someone had taught me, both technical and psychological, thirty years ago. There are exercises, tactics, strategies and solid information that will make your journey smoother. It is a bit like getting decent boots if you want to take a serious long hike: well-fitting boots won't make you fit, won't stop you getting lost, won't make the gradient of the long hills any gentler, but they will make the whole expedition safer, more comfortable and infinitely more pleasurable.

There are parts of creative writing that probably cannot be taught: you do need to find in yourself that odd mixture of inner spark, deep greedy desire and willingness to put in the work that we usually call 'talent'. But there are lots of other parts that are perfectly teachable, because they are perfectly *learnable*. And if you want to learn those things a book is a very good way of doing so.

There is, however, a much more common reason for people seeking a book – or in some cases more and more books – as though somewhere there were a magic spell and if they could only find it everything would be easy. This reason is humility.

Humility and the writer

There are, when it comes to writing, two sorts of humility. There is the good sort: you read something, by someone else – a sentence, a paragraph or two, a way of tackling something, a single perfectly chosen word – and even occasionally a whole book – and you think, 'Wow – that is so good; that is just right, this person is such a good writer.' And if the writing has any connection to the sort of writing you feel you want to do yourself, you will quickly find yourself thinking, 'I wish I could write as well as that.' This is proper, healthy humility and so long as it makes you ambitious rather than envious it is a good and necessary feeling. It encourages aspiration and hard work; it inspires you to think harder about the art and technique of writing; and it also offers you a real pleasure. One of the most interesting things students have said to me at the end of a creative writing course is how much more they get out of *reading*: the story and the emotional content and the beauty and the perception are still there, but a recognition of the author's skill and control is an added bonus. The wise person who is new to writing will want to read more and more, and read more and more carefully, because it offers occasions for this sort of humility.

But there is a second sort of humility that is totally negative and useless. It is also wrong-headed. This is the humility that leads a person to say, 'I haven't got anything to say. My life is too boring, I can't think of anything original, no one wants to read about me and my world; it is all too dull. I want to write so I must read all these books so that I can get a point of view, find some ideas and material, and discover something to say.'

This is total nonsense. But it lies very deep: too many of us were brought up not to 'show off', not to think we were anything special, to be 'good team players'. Nonetheless you don't have to dig very far to realise that – at least with writing – it is entirely false. Most of the great novels are about ordinary daily lives – boy meets girl; grown-ups have children; people meet and chat about the weather, and fall in love and go shopping and get old. Jane Austen once wrote: 'Three or four families in a country village is the very thing to work on.' The whole charm of *Bridget Jones's Diary* is that the heroine is so ordinary – and lives an ordinary urban life with all the problems that every other young woman living a contemporary urban life has. Even wild

...you need to find in yourself that odd mixture of spark, deep desire and willingness to put in the work

books of high adventure and complex plots usually depend on the reader recognizing the characters and their emotions as being somehow just like everyone else's. What makes writing work is very seldom the bizarre situation, but the ability to write accurately and meaningfully about the sorts of things that everyone can recognize. It is the writing not the writer's experience that finally matters.

My agent once said to me that she had never encountered a story so good that bad writing did not make it dull and equally there was no subject so dull that good writing could not make it fascinating. Think of *Cod* by Mark Kurlansky – an international best seller about the history of the codfish.

You have something to say

It is total nonsense in another way too. Of course you have a unique point of view. Of course your life is subtly different from everyone else's. Every single human being who has ever been alive in the world has a unique point of view. If you look at something and then describe exactly what you see it will be different from everyone else's description of the same object.

The you who looks and then describes is unique – even if the object is absolutely familiar, dull and well known, your eyes and your brain will bring to the task of looking at it a whole history that is individual, unique and special. Everybody who reads that description will have their own looking informed – their future description will be informed and changed by yours.

There is an amusing exercise to demonstrate this:

Exercise 2 'Unique point of view' test

☞ You will need a camera – a digital camera makes the whole exercise much simpler – and a group of willing participants.

☞ The group chooses an object. It should be something specific, well known to everyone, perfectly ordinary and not far away, although it is better not to choose something in the same room. Something like a particular tree, car or house is the sort of thing to select.

☞ Over the next hour or so everyone in the group, using the same camera, has to take a single picture of the chosen object. Every picture will be a bit different – taken from a slightly different distance or from a slightly different angle. Each picture of this ordinary old thing will be unique, because it will be the unique choice of each photographer.

Every photographer has their own unique point of view – even when they are using the same camera, and photographing the same scene on the same day. If that is true just for a group of amateur photographers, how much more true is it going to be with writing? Language offers deeper choices than almost any other art form: vocabulary and grammar (words and sentences) and angle and structure. A camera can only photograph what is actually there; language allows you to describe things that are not there (you can add a bird to the tree you photographed) and even things that could not be there (you can place a dragon in the tree you photographed).

You are very special. There is nobody exactly like you in the whole world.

Since the beginning of time there has never been anyone exactly like you. Nobody has your fingerprints, nor your mind-prints, your personal experiences, your way of seeing the world, your psychology and your exact language. You are unique.

So there is no need at all for that second form of humility. It is a little trick that our lazy minds play on us. As you proceed with your writing you will learn just how many subtle reasons we can all come up with to stop us writing. I have come to believe that there is a part in all of us that is actually afraid of our own creativity – that wants to suppress and silence the other part of us which knows perfectly well that we do have something to say and will feel empowered and liberated if we can get it down on paper.

I am fascinated by these tricks of the mind. I will try and describe as many of them as I can in the chapters ahead. Try and see them as warning signs, like those road signs that tell you there are sheep or bumps or dangerous bends on the road ahead.

Everyone is creative

All you really have to do, then, is to look at something until you can truly see it. Good seeing leads to good writing – whether you are seeing something real and concrete 'out there' or something in your 'mind's eye', something you have made up. The two are very nearly the same. On the whole it is easier to practise on actual concrete objects because they have a sort of solidity that means you can check up on them, but all seeing is processed in the brain whether it is imaginary or actual.

Nonetheless we all know that sometimes we write something down and it comes out 'dead' – it is trite or dull or meaningless. What has gone wrong? There are a number of possibilities. Three of the most common though are:

❖ sloppy looking – you have not truly and honestly looked at (or listened to, or thought about or felt) the thing you want to write about. You have seen what you thought was there or what you wanted to be there. You do not need a snap shot, or a sketch; you need a portrait, a full and intricate study. Go and look again.

❖ showing off – that is using what you think is a fancy way of saying what you see, a kind of literary pretentiousness, rather than using your own unique viewpoint.

❖ not trusting yourself about what you see or not believing that it is really worth recording.

One of the most important things this book sets out to do is to try and train its readers in some tactics for overcoming these three central problems. They are technical problems not moral or personal ones, and that is why you can learn ways of dealing with them.

They are not fundamentally problems with your 'creativity'. Everyone is creative.

Human beings are creative animals. In fact everyone is creative most of the time. Every day, every hour we make something new out of what is around us.

At the most basic level, just drawing air into our lungs (or even having it pumped into our lungs by a machine) and expelling it involves us in a complex creative act. We take the air in, we process it, we change it into something new and we put it back into the world. Now there is oxygen in our blood cells and nitrogen in the atmosphere. We are alive. That is impressive.

The trouble is that the phrase 'everyone is creative' has become a cliché. The more we say it, the less it means and the less we do about it – as we can see in the school curriculum. Although we say, 'everyone is creative' we do not do much about developing the skills that would make people more able to enjoy their own creativity and to share it with other people. Of course nitrogen/oxygen separation is 'interesting' and creative but it is not exactly original.

I have been trying to convince you that you do indeed have a unique view of the world, and one that could be valuable for the rest of us to learn about. Now I want to move on and think about how we can use our natural creative skills to make that unique viewpoint available to a wider audience through writing.

Put simply, that is what creative writing is.

The nature of art

Some creative activities are personal, even private. The ones that can speak to a wider audience than just ourselves, or our immediate social circle, are the ones that are called 'art'.

For example, if I cook my beloved a meal, or I write my beloved a love poem these are both creative acts. But if someone else comes and eats the meal my beloved will not be able to enjoy it (or even eat it). If someone comes and reads the love poem though, my beloved will still have it – in fact it may make both of us famous for centuries. The person who took it will also have it, and will be able to pass it on to more lovers. If it is a decent love poem, even if its origins were very personal and true to my own unique experience of one specific human being, it will speak to a wider audience, it will have a life of its own, it will enrich other human lives perhaps for a very long time, and in very different circumstances from those I wrote it in. The poet, therefore, is not more creative than the cook, but is arguably more artistic.

How we learn to use language

With most forms of art you have to learn quite a lot of technique before you can create anything very exciting, but we all learned to use language creatively years and years ago. A mysterious thing happens to almost all children, usually when they are around eighteen months to two years old. Up to this point, they may have learned some words by copying the people around them, or babbled in a way that had the apparent characteristics of a language.

Child psychologists do not quite know what happens next, but suddenly these children can make brand new sentences, remarkably correct as to grammar and construction, that *they have never heard before*. The simplest example is the way they learn to attach the preposition 'my' to something that has always been named 'your'. Very few infants will have heard a grown-up say 'my teddy' or 'my mummy'. They will have heard 'your teddy' and 'my job' or 'my baby'. The first time they put together words like this, something astonishing is happening: they have created a new sentence, and they have communicated their meaning to another person.

Once they have made that leap most children develop language skills at an astronomical rate. By the time they are two and a half they have a vocabulary of several hundred words; they have a pretty complex grammar – including different tenses; and they have the capacity to describe things they do not know the word for. When my daughter, at about this age, first saw a fountain she said, 'Look, a water puff' – perhaps her first metaphor. This is 'creative speaking'.

The language of three-year-olds is constantly fascinating (even if exhausting). It is original, vivid, experimental and exploratory. They are constantly expanding the functions of their language and working out what they can do with it – self-expression, learning, gaining attention, understanding their world, getting what they want, making

...you have a unique view of the world and one that could be valuable for the rest of us to learn about

people laugh, making people angry, comforting themselves and others.

So you've done it once. As you start your own creative writing you are just doing again what you did so brilliantly all those years ago. If you look at what best encourages a child to talk you will be able to draw up a list of the basic equipment you will need for your writing.

❖ Toddlers need good examples of language use. Babies who do not have a lot of language in their environment will not develop it on their own. This is not because they need to copy it exactly, but so they can understand what it is for. Beginner writers (and indeed experienced writers too) need books. You need to read and read attentively – as attentively as three-year-olds listen to what concerns them (in their view this does not usually include bossy instructions and discussions about bedtime!). *A regular habit of reading is essential.* If you are serious about writing you need to be serious about reading.

❖ Early talkers need to be heard. They need to get some response; they need attention and respect for their efforts. However, when you begin writing you usually have to be your own reader. You have to keep a careful record of what you write and you need to re-read it, go back to it, respond to it and treat it with attention and respect. The simplest way to do this is to keep a notebook. A better way to do it is to keep several notebooks – one that is small and discreet should go with you everywhere, at all times. You should copy anything that you write in it into a larger notebook, which ideally stays in your writing place – for you to revisit regularly – and never goes anywhere. Some people use a folder in their word processor as their 'large' notebook but do remember to back up your notes regularly on discs in case of mishap.

❖ Beginner talkers need things to talk about. They need stimulation and new experiences. These do not have to be at all dramatic; a trip to the shop will do nicely. Failing anything else they will ask endless 'why' and 'what' questions as a substitute for direct experiences. Beginner writers need things to write about. Remember that you are your own adult here – give your writer new experiences. Keeping a diary of daily experiences is one way of doing this. Personally, I keep a scrapbook. If the notebook is for things you write, the scrapbook is for things you might write about. I use a box file for this, because you can put anything in it – downloaded pages from the web, clippings from newspapers and magazines, lists of interesting books, but also (which is the advantage of the box) things that aren't simply printed; photographs, postcards and so on. I've got some sweet wrappers in my scrapbook at the moment, some bits of wool in various odd colours, three striped pebbles and a button badge that says 'Blessed are the cracked for they shall let in the light'.

❖ Early-years talkers need space and time. As well as needing a 'language-rich environment' they also need one-to-one time, without too much external stimulation, to work on their talking skills, to inquire and think and brood and struggle to express themselves. Early-years writers need that even more – because they usually have more distractions and pressing engagements than a toddler does. If you possibly can you need to choose a place and a time which you can dedicate to writing.

You will discover, as you go on, what the minimum time you can usefully deploy is. (You are unlikely to discover the maximum time you can spare for writing for several years, if ever. It is rare to get the opportunity to find out.) I know writers who write in cafés, at elegant desks and in the garden shed. I don't know any writers who, at least when they started, did not have a place which was specifically *for writing.* And a time: it does not have to be every day, but it needs to be regular. You need to go there even if you don't think you have got anything to write that day, and you have to stay there for however long you have appointed even if you don't write anything.

❖ Children need permission to experiment. They do not develop fluent language skills if someone is waiting to pounce on their every error, to correct them and chivvy them and tell them how to 'say it properly'. Give your fledgling, internal writer the same permission. It is most unlikely that you will produce *War and Peace* or even a bestselling detective novel straight off. It is very likely that many of your earliest efforts will be distinctly mediocre (some of your later efforts will be too, believe me). No one would try and run a marathon without doing some basic training. Experiment and failure is training for the writer. Do not let that censor-in-your-head anywhere near your writing space and time. Most importantly do not let any censoring go on *before* you have even written something down. Be tolerant, patient and generous.

Necessary equipment

❖ Based on the successful adventure with language that you made all those years ago, here is a summary of the minimum basic equipment you will need to get started on this similar though different journey.

* Three printed books. Ideally a book you read as a child; a novel you haven't read yet but have heard about; and some poetry. (I hope you will have more than three already. This is the economy kit.)

* Three notebooks. A big one (A4 size); a pocket sized one; one with a beautiful cover. (The big one can be a word processor folder if you prefer.) You will need to explore exactly what combination suits you best, but this is a good starting point.

* A box file, drawer, or other appropriate holder for your scrapbook.

* A place you can write, undisturbed by either yourself or other people.

* A clear timetable that you believe you can stick to.

* Some cheap paper (or the reverse sides of used paper) that you can experiment on without inhibitions about waste.

* A generous heart.

Getting used to your equipment

Here are some exercises to help you get used to your equipment. They aren't real writing exercises, but more like the stretches we are supposed to do at the beginning of a serious physical training session.

❖ Go to a good stationery shop. Note how many different types and styles of notebook there are: spiral bound, top and sides; lined, unlined; hardback, floppy; all sorts of sizes; all sorts of covers and designs. Choose at least two that are different from each other. Also choose at least two different sorts of writing tool: roll-tip, graphite pencil, felt-tip; broad or fine nib; red, blue, black (unless you are very strongly drawn to it I'd avoid yellow because it doesn't show up well on a white page of paper). There are also quill and fountain pens, children's coloured crayons, charcoal sticks and about a hundred different fonts for word processors.

❖ As soon as possible after you get home, write in each of the notebooks, with each of the pens. See which combination seems to suit you best. ('Suits you best' in this context usually means, 'gives you most pleasure'.)

Creating a writing environment

❖ Look around your house and ask yourself where you will do your writing. In an ideal world it will be somewhere that you can set aside solely for writing, and which will be out of sight and out of sound of anyone else who shares your space with you. It will also be somewhere that you can safely leave your work and any mess that it has made. However we do not live in an ideal world. You may have to decide that the kitchen table is the best place available. You may need to work on a computer that other people also use. Don't worry about this – great writing has been done under these and far less promising conditions. Do however make very clear to anyone whose business it may be that, in addition to whatever else happens

You have to give inspiration a chance, a time and a place to visit you here, this is your writing space. In the case of a household computer I would recommend setting up a new user identity with a password that only you know; this creates the same privacy that an office, with a lockable door, would give you. A timetable for all its users would avoid a lot of the arguments that inevitably come about from a shared computer, too. It is also worth considering if there is somewhere outside the house that might be better. J.K. Rowling famously wrote the earliest of the Harry Potter books in a café; there are also garden sheds, public libraries and friends' houses.

❖ Take a large sheet of paper and draw up a timetable of your day or week or even – if your life is complicated – of your whole month. When are you going to do this writing? You will need some clear and regular time. If there do not seem to be a reasonable number of solid hours then either you will have to abandon the writing or give up something else: it is as simple as that. (A number of beginning writers with busy schedules have discovered that the easiest thing to give up is the first or last hour of their night's sleep. Those hours tend to be quiet, peaceful and uninterrupted.) Whatever timetable you create you will not stick to it – this is a fact of life. You will need to be flexible, tolerant of yourself and other people, realistic and optimistic. Nonetheless you need that schedule: like Mount Everest it is *there*. You have to give inspiration a chance, a time and a place to visit you. If you aren't there, ready and waiting, inspiration will almost certainly pack its bags and move on. Keep the schedule in your notebook; put the designated writing hours into your diary. If necessary give a copy of it to anyone who may feel they have a right to your time.

❖ Look at the place you have decided to make your writing space. Think about how it feels and looks and will be used. Buy, or move from elsewhere, something lovely to put in the space. Good ideas might be a good quality light; a pot plant or a vase for cut flowers; an 'executive toy' to fiddle with; a new mouse mat if you are a computer user; a comfortable chair cushion.

Starting the scrapbook

❖ Read through an issue of your local newspaper. Clip out two stories from it – one that you find funny and one that you find intriguing. Put them in your scrapbook.

❖ Look through some old glossy magazines. Clip out three pictures of people whose faces look interesting (not people whom you know or know about). Put them in your scrapbook.

❖ If you are on the web, use your search engine to find a new fact – some true thing you did not know before, but are glad to learn. Print it off. Put this in your scrapbook.

❖ Next time you are out of your house, watch and listen. When you get home, write down one thing you heard someone say or saw someone do that piqued your curiosity. Put this in your scrapbook.

Using your writing space

❖ Sit where you plan to sit when you write and read a book – any book – for the length of time you have decided to make your writing session.

❖ Sit where you plan to sit when you write and do nothing at all
– absolutely nothing – for the length of time you have decided
to make your writing session. Think, daydream, imagine you
are a writer.

❖ *Do not write anything.*

Now what?

Chapter 1 Travelling

This is the unnerving bit. Unplug the telephone; turn off the doorbell; threaten anyone who might disturb you; proceed to your writing space.

Start writing.

There is something very strange about writing. Almost all writers develop cunning internal strategies to evade the actual physical business of *writing*. But if you look honestly at your own excuses and techniques you will probably see that they are strategies to evade *starting to write*. Because oddly enough once you are actually doing it, writing has an almost compulsive quality. You will find that you lose your sense of time, that you bitterly resent interruptions, and that there is a seductive power in the half written paragraph that was unimaginable when you first confronted the blank sheet of paper. The hurdle is *starting*. It is undeniably hard, it can feel overwhelming, but it is absolutely the only way that you can reach the place you are trying to get to – inside the writing itself.

So, I repeat: unplug the telephone; turn off the doorbell; threaten anyone who might disturb you; proceed to your writing space.

Start writing.

Generating your material

In one sense that is what it boils down to, but of course it is not quite that simple.

There is something you need to understand, not just intellectually but emotionally. If you are a cook and you want to invent a new recipe you gather the ingredients as well as the utensils (the oven, the mixing bowls and so on). If you are a potter and you want to make a bowl, you go out and buy your clay. If you are a painter you do not

the way

feel you are obliged to mix all your own paints and weave the canvas before you begin. You start, in short, with the materials you need as well as the tools. Writing is different: there are no materials. In the last chapter I was describing the tool-kit you will need – not the materials. Before you can cook up your great work you need to generate some material, some ingredients for yourself. Notes, exercises, experimental sentences and first drafts need to be seen as the untreated material of the future work.

When the cook takes the shopping out of the carrier bag and puts it on the table, when the potter digs a lump of clay out of the clay bin and slaps it onto the wheel, they do not think the work is done. Raw vegetables and meat are not a casserole; a lump of clay is not a bowl. An outline, some brilliant images, a first draft is not a work of literature: it is the crude material that you, the writer, are going to work on and from which you hope and plan to produce a piece of writing. This means that you cannot expect a first draft to be great writing any more than you would expect raw flour to be tasty. You have to work your material like any other artist does. The material of writing is language, written language. Like the cook you have to choose good ingredients and you have to understand how they work and how they might taste when they have been 'cooked'. But above all you have to work them, work on them and with them and through them.

So getting started is not, in the first instance, about creating a great work of literature: it is about collecting together some ingredients, some clay, some materials. Even if you think you know what it is you want to write this gathering of material remains important. Your notebook and your scrapbook are places to store your material – the clay bin, the refrigerator of your writing. Value them – not as literature in themselves but as the storehouse of literature.

...a first draft is not a work of literature: it is the crude material that you are going to work on

Finding a way in

In a sense therefore, as you start, it really hardly matters what you write so long as you do write. Everyone is different and therefore everyone has a different 'way in'. What follows are a few of the many ways that different writers have found for getting inside the writing. I recommend that in your early writing days you try lots of them. Imagine that your own voice is locked in a cellar and you are outside the door. These exercises are a bunch of keys – you will have to try them each in turn until you find the one that will let you in. (And if ever, later on, you feel completely stuck come back to this chapter and try the exercises again – not just the ones that worked last time, but some of the others as well.)

Exercise 3 Write about a colour

➪ Pick a colour. (Start with a fairly common one.) Write the word for this colour at the top of your page – e.g. BLUE.

➪ Write for fifteen minutes about blue. Objects, moods, memories – *anything* that relates to blue.

➪ Do not stop writing for more than ten seconds at a time. Do not read what you have written. If one train of thought fades away, simply put a full stop and start a new paragraph with something else.

➪ Do not worry if you find that what you are writing moves away from being about blue. This is good: your subconscious has been triggered; let it have its own way.

➪ Do not worry if you find that you are writing obsessively

about only one idea of blue (e.g. the sky or your favourite shirt). This is good: your concentration has been attracted; stay with it.

☞ Do not worry if you find that your ideas are scattered, and that your paragraphs are only one sentence long, or even only one word long. This is good: your mind is making fast, creative associations; keep going.

☞ After fifteen minutes you *must* stop. A kitchen timer, or other alarm bell, may prove useful. Now read what you have written. Once. Do not correct anything, even obvious spelling mistakes. Do not throw the paper away. Keep it for future reference.

☞ If your committed writing time is longer than twenty minutes (fifteen for the writing and five for the reading and filing) don't stop: pick another colour and repeat the process.

You can do this exercise with almost any word. Colours are a helpful starting point because they have a goodly number of associations for most people. Moreover they will probably be *sensory* rather than intellectual associations. Try the same exercise with more abstract words (like freedom, hope or imagination) and you may well find that you start producing little school essays – at this point this is not what you want. You are trying to explore the territory of your *own* language and your *own* creativity. There is a hidden schoolteacher in all of us lurking around and longing to put a red pencil through our essay writing. She, or he, will have less access to your punctuation if you work for the moment on something different.

It is also worth remembering that this sort of free association (written or spoken) is used by psychologists and psychoanalysts to unearth repressed and painful material. Unless you are already skilled in using these approaches I suggest that you do not use emotions, or emotionally loaded words (like anger, love or father). Later, when you are more at home with the depths of your own creativity and the power of language you may well want to come back to this exercise with more potent and perilous words. These are early days; little will be gained by upsetting yourself and even less by scaring yourself.

Exercise 4 Write about an object

☞ Choose an object – something small enough to hold. Again, something ordinary or common usually works best.

☞ Concentrate on it for three or four minutes. Look at it. Feel it, smell it, taste it (if appropriate!) listen to it – listen to its silence too. The reason why a common object is useful this time is because you have to put aside all the generalities you know about 'pencils' or 'apples' or 'stones' and concentrate on *this* one – you honour your own uniqueness by honouring its uniqueness. There is no other pencil or apple or stone exactly like this one in the world. (The uniqueness of a single coin or cigarette can be harder to perceive of course, but the principle remains.)

☞ Put it aside, where you can't see or touch it.

☞ Write about it. Try and describe it so that someone who has not seen it could pick it out from a group of similar objects.

Write about it as though you loved it. (Mothers know about this – they can pick out their own newborn baby from a whole nursery of babies whom everyone else finds more or less indistinguishable.)

☞ When you have described it fully, pick it up again, and compare your writing with the object itself.

☞ Ask yourself:

Have I honoured its uniqueness? Check whether more general ideas about this type of object have crept into your writing in ways that come between the object and the reader (in this case you).

Have I seen and remembered it properly? It is, for instance, very easy to describe a nice red apple as 'rosy' – but have you ever actually seen a rose that was the colour of *this* apple?

Have I described it fully? Is there anything else you could say about it – or indeed about yourself seeing and writing about it?

☞ Put it aside – write about it again, either adding on to the description you have already written or starting afresh if you prefer. Try both. Whichever method you feel most satisfied by, do not throw away anything from the first description. Keep it.

☞ Repeat this looking and then writing process, with the same object, for the whole of your allotted writing session.

☞ If you have chosen an object you can keep, keep it! Put it in your scrapbook, or – especially if you were pleased with your writing – set it out somewhere you can see it, ideally in or near your writing space.

There are a number of variations on this exercise:

Ask friends or family members to select the object for you. The next time they do it, ask them to hand it to you while you keep your eyes shut, so that your first impressions of it are not visual: write your exercise using only the other four senses, then look at the object and think about what sight might add to your description.

If you have a companion, another writer or would-be writer, share the exercise. Ideally you want to be together while you do this, but do not discuss the object before you begin. Apart from giving you both encouraging new ideas to develop your own skills it will also underline the point I made in the previous chapter – you will both describe this common domestic thing very differently. You will both have a unique view of the object, and a unique way of describing it.

If you are very near the beginning of your writing journey, I strongly advise you to come to a further agreement with such a companion. Agree in advance that you will listen to each other's description carefully and you will thank each other for the help you have both given – but you will not praise or criticize anything the other one has actually written. Nor will either of you, in any way, apologize for or belittle your own writing. At this stage you are looking for your way – you do not need another voice to interrupt your exploration. That attentive critical listener will be invaluable later – but at present another commenting voice will only create static; the background buzz and fuzz of an imperfectly tuned radio.

A small object is good to start with, because you can get so close to it, and because your writing may well be able to encompass it, but of course you can also do this exercise with larger objects: your pet dog, a tree, the view out of the window. The same rules apply though (as far as is realistic).

Exercise 5 Rewrite a story

Think of a story – not one of your own, but a story you already know. The best sort of story for this exercise is an old one – a fairy story, legend, myth or traditional tale. Best of all is one that you can remember from childhood, but basically you are trying to dig out a story from your memory: do not go and look for the story in books, or re-read it, or 'check the details'.

➣ Rewrite the story 'in your own words'. Keep it simple. Keep it short. Try to avoid explaining too much; just write it as though you were telling it. If your story goes off in its own direction, feel free to follow it.

➣ Relax – try to enjoy the story in the way that you might have enjoyed it as a child. Don't try to be literary, or clever, or funny. *(If it is itself a funny story let it be funny – don't try to be funny yourself. Comic writing is very sophisticated and complex even for those graced with 'natural' verbal wit. If that is where your journey is heading, great, but don't try to run before you are walking steadily.)*

➣ Just write into the story – keep moving forward. Do not go back and read anything you have written until you get to the end.

☞ Read it once. Do not correct anything. Try to feel how it compares with the story you meant to tell. It can be useful to make a note of any strong feelings you have either in your journal or at the bottom of the story itself. Then put it away somewhere safe.

Using newspaper stories

If you followed the recommendations in the opening chapter, you will have a couple of newspaper stories in your scrapbook that have already tickled your imagination. (With a bit of luck you will have gone on adding to this collection, and the other collections I suggested, as well as your own new ones; so you may have a wider selection than the original two.) Read them through, choose one that still has its appeal for you and use that instead of a more traditional story for this exercise.

There are two points to this – one is the simple one of getting you writing, getting you into the practice and pleasure of writing, helping you find your way into that part of yourself that you want to write out of. The other idea is that using already existing stories allows you to write your own stories without the additional effort of making up the plot, deciding what ought to happen and working out the structure. This means you can access your own emotional and writing agenda, without having to worry about the technical scaffolding.

Good journalists are very close to the ancient bards and storytellers – probably closer in many ways than the modern poet or fiction writer. Their narrative technique is similar; their 'eye' or 'ear' for a good story is honed by a very direct reader response; their sense of structure and direction is trained ruthlessly by having to write to a very precise word length and space, and deliver to an absolute deadline. I suggested a local paper (rather than a national one) because they tend to have more items that are simply human interest *stories.* You will not need much background knowledge, nor will you be awed by the scale of the story or the fame of the characters in it. Later, of course, you will want to make up your own stories, or use your own life as a story – this is an exercise for getting started; for finding comfortable ways of generating the crude material you are going to work on and with.

Exercise 6 Writing a portrait

Choose a photograph. Again you should find you have a couple of these in your scrapbook, but if not thumb through a glossy magazine or newspaper until you see a person who interests you – not someone you know, but a stranger whose face or activity attracts your imagination. (Do not ignore advertisements – more often than we might like, the models chosen for this work have faces that are close to our own dreams and aspirations.)

➤ Write about this character. Write anything you can think of. Describe how he or she looks and what is going on in the picture; but also feel free to make up past lives, psychologies, even conversations for your character. Just keep writing. If you write things that are contradictory, or confuse you, or that feel wrong after you have got them down, don't stop, don't cross out and don't correct anything.

➤ What you are trying to explore here, as in the previous exercise, is not so much the art of creating fictional characters (although that will inevitably be part of it) but what is going on in your own imagination – and how that is reflected in what you write. Why does this picture attract you more than other pictures do? What part of yourself, or your life, are you using the character to write about?

☞ As before, when you have written for fifteen minutes, stop. Read what you have written once and then put it away safely. If you are writing by hand, or printing out your work it is quite useful to pin the picture to the writing – so that later you can look more critically at the two together. But if this is not possible then make a note on the writing itself about where to find the picture in case you should need it again.

Provided that you do not feel overawed by the artist's talent or reputation, an even better way to get going on this sort of exercise is to use portraits, or characters from *paintings*. Great painters will already have done something of what you are beginning to try to do: they will have found, or struggled to find, the relationship between their sitter and their own creativity, and then attempted to express that in their own medium – paint. In this sense you will not be working entirely alone, but with the companionship of another creative mind and eye.

This is a particularly interesting exercise if you enjoy modern, less representational art. Writing about a Picasso portrait, for example, and trying to see the sitter as a person is challenging, but it can be very stimulating to your writing.

Using a monologue

A 'monologue' is the technical name for any piece of writing in which one character 'speaks' directly to the reader or audience. Since Alan Bennett's extraordinary and wonderful monologues for television in the 1980s, monologues are sometimes called 'talking heads' – the name of his show. But they do not need to be performed: a great many short stories, poems and even novels are monologues.

Another way of doing this exercise is to write it as a monologue. Imagine what the characters you have chosen would say about themselves. Write it all with 'I': 'I am lying on a green bed. It is annoyingly cold. . .' or whatever comes to your mind as you move it into another body and a different pair of eyes. The writer is looking in, but the character is looking out. When you read it back to yourself after you have finished writing, try and see how and where your own writer's 'I' blends with the fictional 'I' that you are speaking through.

Exercise 7 Describe a recent dream

➡ The idea here is to write from *inside* the dream. Try not to separate the feeling or experience of the dream from the events and images in it. For example, if you write, 'A large hen rushed towards me. It seemed very frightening' you have separated the content of the dream from the experience of the dream. In the experience of the dream you – the dreamer – did not stand aside commenting on your feelings. There was something very scary about that hen within the experience of the dream, which is how you know now, afterwards, that it was frightening. The idea is to write the dream in exactly the way that you dreamed it. Even more important than not separating the feelings from the events, is trying not to abstract a meaning from the events. 'A large hen rushed towards me. It was very frightening. I realise that it represented my mother', separates out all the three main constituents of a dream. The interpretation is interesting but it is not the purpose of the exercise. This is not psychoanalysis. You do not want to explain the dream, but to show it – and to see how well you can capture the whole sensation of your own unique dream world.

You will perhaps notice that the instructions for this exercise are shorter and crisper than the previous suggestions. To be honest this is because I know absolutely nothing about it. I very seldom have, or at least remember, dreams, and when I do they are so mundane it is embarrassing. They tend to lack any emotional content or any interesting images whatsoever. (I like to think this is because my unconscious is allowed full range in my fiction and I don't need to work things out while I'm asleep.)

Nonetheless, I am including this as a way of getting started on your own writing because so many writers do find that notes from their dreaming lives open up their writing, inform their consciousness and inspire their work. Several of them have told me that they actually keep a separate notebook, which lives beside their bed and in which they record their dreams before they even get up in the morning. *(I have tried this – but I still don't have any dreams worth recording!)* If you are aware of having a rich and emotionally complex dream life you too may find this exercise really helpful.

Exercise 8 Keep a journal

➤ Write in it regularly. Treat it as part of your writing time.

➤ The important thing with this sort of journal is to keep it concrete and specific. It can be as detailed as you like. Try for example writing about getting up in the morning or about preparing last night's meal. (Kitchens make remarkably good gyms for writers, because they are multi-sensory: you see, smell, taste, touch and hear all at once – what is the difference between the noise a knife makes slicing through an onion, and chopping up a carrot?

☛ Record precisely what you did and what you felt.

☛ Take a single event of your day – washing, dressing, your walk to work, the weather outside, the furnishing of your living room, a conversation you overheard, a child you saw playing. It hardly matters what – but don't make it abstract, intellectual or 'general'.Don't write about gardens in the springtime; write about this particular bulb spike you noticed breaking the ground. Don't write about how much you hate rush hour traffic; write about the individual cross-looking driver in the car beside yours and his obviously sneering moustache.

☛ Try to recapture the moment of the experience and then write about exactly how it was, how you – you alone with your unique vision and your unique language – perceived and experienced it.

☛ Sometimes people will say that they have 'nothing to write about'. These are precisely the people who need to keep a journal. If they really think that 'nothing happened' all day, then they weren't paying attention. I have already spoken about both seeing and recording/writing: interestingly the two go together. The more you write down what you saw and heard and felt and thought, then the more you will see (and hear, and feel and think). Quite apart from the deep satisfaction that writing can give you, creativity is life enhancing. But you do have to pay attention. A journal entry that says 'Got up, went to work, came home' is *at least* three opportunities missed.

☞ Once you have got started, decide where you will focus your memory's eye. Try not to think too hard about the writing itself. Just write. Scraps of sentences may be enough; a single word may be enough. Take the day or the moment down into the writing and trust yourself.

☞ At the end of the allotted time, stop. Read through what you have written without correcting anything. Date each entry in your journal. Keep it safe.

This business of keeping a journal is very personal. It does not suit every writer, and it is certainly not *necessary* On the other hand it is both a very good way of getting started and a very common practice among established writers. It is almost certainly worth a try – even if you only treat it as a resource for those writing times when you cannot think of anything else to write.

There is some debate about whether your journal and your notebook can or should be the same thing. I personally keep them separate – in my notebook I make notes about things I might want to write, things I want to find out about and very often comments on things I have written. For me a journal is *writing itself* – even though it will never, in the form I write it, appear in public. But many writers don't – they run the two together in what is obviously a very fulfilling way *for them*. You will need to experiment, and I suspect that for all of us what works best changes over time, both because we become more experienced and because we ourselves grow and change. There are no rules here. The important thing is that keeping a journal is one way, and a well-established way, of developing your writing muscles *and* of creating the material (the clay, the ingredients) for the more substantial writing that you want to do.

This is the purpose of all the exercises and tactics I have been describing. The following hints apply to them all more or less equally; they are the fruits of my own experience and the results of talking to other writers and reading biographies and autobiographies.

Hints for getting started

❖ **Planning your sessions in advance**. Many of us find totally spontaneous writing difficult, even scary. I find it useful to decide *in general* how I will use a particular writing session the night before. But only in general: so I might decide that I would work on the 'single word exercise' (Exercise 3) or the 'photograph exercise' (Exercise 6), just so that I don't use up the whole session dithering around and never quite making a commitment to anything. But one central purpose of these exercises is to surprise yourself, so you don't want to think in advance about precisely what words you will write. Don't pick your colour or photograph until the moment you sit down to write.

You may find, as you discover your writing voice, that you develop an instinct about what you need to work on. You may be working on something far beyond these exercises – a whole large piece of work, which not only dictates how you use the session, but dictates what you think about most of the day. But as you start out you want to plan enough to make you feel confident and happy as you go to your writing. There are things inside you that only the act of writing itself will reveal. Don't thwart those still-hidden perceptions and ideas.

❖ **Stopping on time**. In my description of these exercises you may have noticed that I keep on stressing that you should **stop** when your chosen time is up. I know this surprises some people: 'Surely', they think, 'if the inspiration is flowing I should flow with it for as long as I can.' But there are a number of reasons why *in the long term* this will prove the best approach, especially at the beginning. Firstly, if you stop while you are still hungry and excited, it is easier to start again the next time, rather than being left with a sense of weary exhaustion and the feeling you are now 'written out'. Secondly, it is much easier to tame and train that shy, elusive writing self if it knows that there are clear limits to what you expect of it. The analogy here is with physical exercise – you do a set number of push-ups, or run a set number of miles; while this quantity may increase in both duration and intensity as you get fitter, you really do know that it is incremental and progressive: you can't run a whole marathon just because 'you feel like it'. Thirdly, if you neglect other things in your life that you know need doing (eating and sleeping among them) the act of writing will become guilt inducing as opposed to joyful. Fourthly, if you allow yourself to extend one session it is surprisingly easy to reduce the length of the next one – if the stopping point becomes fixed in your mind it will work both ways. And finally, writing within a clearly defined space of time is the very first exercise in structure and pace, which are among the most essential qualities of good writing. There will always be times when stopping writing will be impossible once you have started. But if you develop good habits at the beginning you will be able to ride these glorious waves securely when they come.

❖ **Keeping a commentary.** At the end of several of the exercises I have suggested dating the writing or attaching it in one way or another to its source of inspiration (for example, 'pin the picture to the writing' in Exercise 6). This is the very start of creating a 'commentary'. It gives you a small but real way of linking the world of your writing to the world of your other selves. You need to develop this skill. At the end of every session it is a good idea to make a few notes about the session: did I enjoy this exercise? Did I feel unexpected things coming up? Am I being honest? Was the session, and the writing I did in it, satisfying? Difficult? Disappointing? Exciting? Most people find this very tricky at first, but it can be invaluable both for developing your own sense of writing and for going back to later on so you can see how far you have travelled. I shall come back to this business of the commentary, because it is quite a new idea and I think a very valuable one.

❖ **Reading your material back to yourself.** Again I have recommended this at the end of every exercise. I have also suggested that you make no critical comments or changes to what you have written. (This is particularly important if you are using a computer to write on, because any changes you make will obliterate the original: at least when it's handwritten you can keep both copies.) But the idea of reading back at this stage is simply to discover what you have got – not to change it into something else. Remember the image of the cook: no good cooks 'whip up egg whites into stiff peaks' before deciding what they are going to make with them. You are not proposing to turn this raw material into great literature directly – you are the traveller leafing through brochures; a sculptor

> If you stop writing while you are still hungry and excited, it is easier to start again the next time

inspecting a marble quarry. However, it can be encouraging to remember that the opening sentence, even the opening paragraph, of any new piece of writing is nearly always *dreadful* – it seems to be a bit like knocking up before a game of tennis. You have to write yourself into your writing. So don't stop reading when you see that the first words are complete and total rubbish. I sometimes think that the bit of me that writes is asleep when I am not actually doing it – I have to wake it up and it stumbles itself out on to the page yawning and stretching and bleary-eyed and stupid. Give it time to wake up and shake itself. This is not a beginner's problem, I assure you. The beginner's problem is worrying about it.

❖ **Killing the critic**. *Every single person* who has ever written anything has, at one level or another, had to stamp down hard on the critic inside, that mean-minded, negative-thinking, nasty part of themselves that pops up to say 'You, a writer, who are you kidding?' Stamp on it. Kill it. Shout back. Better still is to negotiate with your inner critic: tell it firmly that you do indeed value its critical impulse and know it will help you eventually – indeed that it will be crucial to the production of anything worth reading – BUT NOT YET.

'This,' you have to tell it firmly, 'is not yet my sort of writing. If you want some writing to get your teeth into then let me get on with learning about what "our" writing will look like. Then you can have a field day, for now – shut up.' It is even worth pointing out to such an internal critic that it has had its way for years – you have put off doing this writing over and over again because of its whingeing and threats. It has failed to kill the desire, the hope and the enthusiasm in you. Now you are going to try a different approach. Use any method that appeals to you – but don't listen to that critic just now.

I hope that this chapter will have given you some tools for getting started. Use them if they feel useful. But remember that no amount of wishful thinking will create a work of literature. Experienced writers will tell you that one of the most irritating things that other people say to us is, 'I've always thought I had a book inside me.'

Books are not inside people – they are inside book covers. Books very precisely have to be *outside* people, and especially outside their writers. An idea for a book is not a book. A book is something that has been written down, pushed out, worked on. In order to write anything, let alone anything good, you need to get your hand moving across a piece of paper or your fingers hopping up and down on a keyboard.

In the end the only sound advice for getting started is: get started.

* Don't worry if it feels like rubbish – you have to clear away and dig through an enormous amount of rubble to find a diamond.

* Don't worry if it isn't any good – it is just raw ingredients.

* Don't worry if you can't see where it's all going – you'll never find out unless you go there with it.

* Don't worry that it may all be a waste of time – it cannot be more of a waste than sitting around wishing you were writing.

Just do it. Write.

Chapter 2 Play with

So, by now you are beginning to develop a writing practice. You are writing. This in itself is exciting. I hope that you are building up your confidence, by a combination of regular writing sessions and the realisation that you are generating your own raw materials.

Somewhere at about this point something else very exciting may also happen – and if it has not happened to you then I am going to try and make it happen. I hope you may be getting curious about the 'science' of your raw material. Back to our cooks for a moment – the ones in the last chapter, who were busy buying and storing the ingredients. When people start learning to cook they tend to think of the meal and follow the instructions, but after a while they tend to get curious – why does flour, fat and heat thicken liquids? What is yeast and how does it work? Why does the recipe tell me to do things in a specific order? These are basic scientific questions.

The equivalent question as you start writing is, 'What is this raw material – how does it work?' The answer (or more precisely one of the answers) is *language*. Words are the atoms of writing, and sentences are the molecules. If you want to take this image further you could also say that letters were the sub-atomic particles of language. A group of words, each made up of a string of letters, together with other 'language signs' like punctuation, combine in very particular ways to make sentences. *By sentences I mean clumps of language which carry meaning – I am not talking here about correct grammar and how every sentence must have a subject and a verb.* The sentences strung together like pearls on a cord are what make your writing – not your great ideas, nor even your unique voice, but these little language molecules.

So in a very profound sense, writing, if it is going to be effective and meaningful, needs not only the courage and honesty and hard work I have already talked about, but also a cunning and knowing

language

manipulation of language. It is always easier to be thoughtful and knowledgeable about something we find interesting, easiest of all about something that we love. So in this chapter I want to stir up your interest, your curiosity and your love, about language itself, what it is, how it works and what it can do. I want to help you fall in love with language. I should quickly say here that I am not a professional linguist. In this area I am a true amateur – but I make no apologies for this because the word 'amateur' basically means 'a lover' (from the Latin word *amo* – I love).

This of course is where the scientific imagery breaks down, because language is deeply mysterious. Its origins are mysterious, as every anthropologist and linguist agrees. How it works is mysterious, as every educationalist and psychologist agrees. What you can do with it is mysterious, as every writer and reader knows. The whole issue is bathed in mystery. In some ways this is encouraging, because it means that the subject will never lose its fascination; in some ways it is frustrating, because you will never get it completely under control, or feel that you can command it.

The power of language

The first mystery, the one that underlies all the other mysteries about language, is that it is so *powerful*. Here is a short list of concrete nouns – the sorts of words that name actual things. Read through the list, saying each word aloud and pausing for a moment after each of them:

chair
home
tree
apple

diamond
slonery
pencil

As you say, or even see, each word you will almost certainly have found it impossible not to have some thought or image about the thing that the word names.

Your response to the word 'slonery' will be particularly interesting because I made it up. However, I suspect if nothing else you will have experienced some irritation; you may even, by association, have given it some meaning.

These are concrete nouns. However, if you try the same thing with a list of abstract nouns you will discover that they also provoke some thoughts or ideas or feelings:

mathematics
love
democracy
creativity
power
education
goodness
envy

The same is true if you use verbs or adjectives. Like magic they bring the object or action, or a range of ideas associated with them, into your mind without any effort. Indeed the effort becomes necessary if you try to avoid this magical claiming of your imagination and emotions. You can try the old children's game of spending a whole minute NOT thinking about 'pink elephants'. It is impossible – as soon as the words are there, your mind cannot help leaping upon them and making them into something recognizable.

Language is arbitrary

What is truly mysterious about this is that there is now a general agreement that the word, or name, given to any object is arbitrary. There is no actual association between the word 'dog' and the furry animal with a wet nose that barks. If that connection really existed it would be impossible for there to be more than one language in the world. In fact when a French person says '*chien*' or a Malay person says '*anjing*' similar images will come to their minds as when you think 'dog'. D-O-G is just an arbitrary collection of symbols that we in the English speaking community, have somehow agreed will perform this mental trick. In some, though by no means all, cases there is a history of how we came to agree that this particular word would represent this particular object, but it remains peculiar and confusing that something so chancy and random should have such enormous power over our free wills.

It is worth bearing in mind that the letters themselves are arbitrary – there is nothing in the shape or history of, say, the letter **A** that obliges it to make an 'a' sound. Three random symbols – a curvy half moon: **C**; a triangle with legs: **A**; and a stick with a flat top: **T**; get put together and that makes us all think of a furry semi-domesticated animal about which we may have quite strong emotional feelings. This is fascinating, strange and mysterious.

Interestingly, the more we learn about languages that use pictograms rather than obviously phonic letters – like Chinese or Egyptian hieroglyphs – the more we become aware that they too are arbitrary. They aren't little tiny representations, but are full of phonics, puns, and other forms of abstract arbitrary assigned meaning. If this interests you at all, in *The Just So Stories*, Kipling tells two lovely little tales about the invention of writing: 'How the First Letter was Written' and 'How the Alphabet was Made'. Here Taffy, a Neolithic girl, and her father invent the alphabet by simplifying drawings – so that the L is a broken spear and the S is a snake. This, as we now know, is complete rubbish but it is charming and touching. Moreover it demonstrates something even more mysterious about language – as well as using words to summon up things that do exist, we can also use them to summon up things that do not exist, like a 'unicorn' or a totally bogus history of the invention of the alphabet.

It is because of this power in language that we are able both to create new things and to tell lies. Like everything powerful and mysterious, language needs to be treated with respect, care and integrity.

Language and meaning

This summoning effect is what we mean when we say that language has 'meaning'. A sound or group of sounds produces certain patterns in our heads – more or less irresistibly. In some cases the meaning can be fairly general and dispersed: if I say 'red' there is a wide range of things I could be suggesting and each of us will probably see a slightly different 'red'; if I say 'scarlet' I will have narrowed down the range of possible meanings; if I say 'pillar-box red' (to anyone who knows British pillar boxes) my meaning will be very precise indeed, even if I am talking about a coat rather than a pillar box. If I say someone has red hair it will also be reasonably precise but will summon up a very different group of reds. And if I say, 'She was so furious that she saw red,' it will conjure up a totally different sort of meaning – though it may be just as precise.

Meaning is, for most people, the first and principal use of language – to say what we mean and to have that meaning understood by others. But as we look at the whole subject of creative writing in more detail we will come to realise that meaning is not isolated within the individual word: it is developed and enriched by the context in which the word appears.

A core skill in great creative writing is the manipulation and management of that context.

Every word, as you write it down, carries with it far more than its crude 'literal' meaning. All words, as well as that meaning, have other more secret ways of influencing the reader. Words have a meaning – and, among other things, they also have:

❖ A **shape.** The way words occupy the page.

❖ A **sound**. The reader hears in the mind what they would sound like if they were spoken. They have this sound because most of us speak before we read and the sound lingers in our heads. This is not true for everyone; deaf people whose 'first language' is one of the sign languages have a second shape, a gestural shape or sign instead of a sound. There are some 'lost' languages that scholars know how to read: they can extract meaning from the written words, but do not know how to speak them – they do not know the sound of the language.

❖ An **atmosphere** or 'register'. As well as a literal meaning individual words have different degrees of formality and are more suited to different occasions. The three words 'tummy', 'stomach' and 'abdomen' would be examples of this: they mean more or less exactly the same thing, but have distinctly different atmospheres.

* A **rhythm.** This is most obvious when words are put in to groups, but each word has an internal rhythm as well.

* A **history**. Most of the words we use do not appear magically from nowhere but come with a huge subtext of origin and older usage and implication. The history of words is called etymology and is in itself a fascinating study, but knowing at least a little about it is a vital tool for a writer.

I think this is really important, as well as great fun, so I am now going to elaborate on each of these elements of language, and suggest some ways you can develop and deepen your own understanding of how to use them in your writing.

THE SHAPE OF WORDS

All words have a shape on the page – at the most basic level they are each longer or shorter than others. Most adult readers read words they know by their shape, rather than by their 'phonic' values – the sounds that their individual letters make (English spelling makes this a vital skill, but it is also part of the way the human brain absorbs and interprets the visual symbols that are written words – whatever language is being used). Simple sentences, especially ones that are already known to the reader, are also read by their shape on the page rather than by the individual words. Short, well-known words in short, simple sentences are therefore easier and quicker to read than long, obscure words in long, grammatically complicated sentences.

On the whole the present fashion is for simpler and more direct 'easier' writing – but the cunning writer can manipulate the reader's feelings and should not be ashamed to do so. You can slow the reader down, make them pay closer attention, work harder, speed up and get excited just by choosing the words and sentence shapes you deploy thoughtfully. Writing can use the shapes on the page as one way of compensating for all the gestures, facial expressions and changes of volume and pitch that spoken language uses to convey mood and emotional meaning. We all know the expression, 'It wasn't what you said, it was the way that you said it.' The shape of words can act like that in writing.

This is usually easier to see in poetry. One obvious difference between poetry and prose is that they make very different shapes on the page. In poetry it matters where the lines end, whereas in prose you usually do not want the reader to notice where the lines end; you want them to move straight on to the next line without losing their concentration and drive. The space the poem occupies on the page is part of its meaning and mood. The convention of 'line breaks' is one way that poets have devised to make people read the words rather differently from the way they read prose. Even in prose though the length of the words, the sentences, the paragraphs and the chapters affect how the reader absorbs the writing.

In *Alice in Wonderland*, Lewis Carroll has a famous poem, 'The Mouse's Tale'. In it, Carroll plays a complex language game. Part of it is about the space on the page and the look of the poem as a mouse's curling tail. It is impossible to say this poem aloud and get its full delightful effect: when you read the book to a child, for example, you have to show them the page.

Carroll's intention is both ironic and humorous, but the same sort of trick can be done perfectly seriously, as George Herbert did in his poem 'Easter Wings'. The two poems are over the page.

Fury said to a mouse,
That he met in the
house, 'Let us
both go to law:
I will prosecute
you – Come, I'll
take no denial;
We must have
a trial: For
really this
morning I've
nothing to do.'
Said the mouse
to the cur,
'Such a trial,
dear Sir, With
no jury or
judge, would
be wasting
our breath.'
'I'll be
judge, I'll
be jury,'
Said cunning
old Fury:
'I'll try
the whole
cause, and
condemn
you
to
death.'

In 'Easter Wings', Herbert has made the poem in the shape of angels' wings. The two shortest lines even have 'poor' and 'thin' in them to help make his point further.

> LORD, *who createdst man in wealth and store,*
> *Though foolishly he lost the same,*
> *Decaying more and more,*
> *Till he became*
> *Most poor:*
> *With thee*
> *O let me rise*
> *As larks, harmoniously,*
> *And sing this day thy victories:*
> *Then shall the fall further the flight in me.*
>
> *My tender age in sorrow did begin:*
> *And still with sicknesses and shame*
> *Thou didst so punish sin,*
> *That I became*
> *Most thin.*
> *With thee*
> *Let me combine*
> *And feel this day thy victory*
> *For, if I imp my wing on thine,*
> *Affliction shall advance the flight in me.*

This sort of writing is called concrete, emblematic or visual poetry. If you think you might find it interesting to write this sort of thing – of which there are many contemporary examples – you can look on the web for more information.

Even if you do not aspire in this particular direction you can develop your own sense of the shape of language by experimenting with concrete poetry.

Exercise 9 Concrete poetry

➡ Select any object that has a clearly defined shape. (A crane for example is a very good choice, because it is mainly constructed of straight lines; and has that long horizontal section at or near the top. Nothing much else is the shape of a crane. A butterfly would be an interesting choice. A bath sponge however would be an awkward choice, because each individual sponge has an amorphous shape, and as a general category bath sponges can in fact come in all sorts of shapes.)

➡ Write a description of it that fits into that shape.

➡ You are not allowed to change the size of your writing, or your font, in order to make the words fit into your chosen design. Nor are you allowed to change the spaces between words. You must change the shape of the words themselves.

➡ There is not a great deal of point to the exercise unless you take care that the description and the shape of the writing strengthen each other.

➡ Unlike the exercises in the previous chapter, you will probably need to 'fiddle about' with this bit of writing, adjusting the words so that the poem describes the object, makes sense and fits the shape, all at the same time. So this exercise will also introduce you to some elementary editing skills.

☛ This is a game – you do not have to create great literature. You are just exploring one aspect of the words you going to use to construct great literature.

THE SOUND OF WORDS

Most of us are probably more aware of how different words *sound* than we are of what shape they have. I think this is because listening, rather than reading, is the way that most of us first acquire language. In fact, at some subliminal level, we 'hear' the sounds of words even when we read silently. This is why we are happy to feel that 'cough' and 'plough' do not rhyme, but that 'cough' does rhyme with 'off' and 'plough' with 'cow'. 'Cough' and 'plough' have the same shape, but not the same sound – our sense of rhyme is not visual but aural.

Moreover, although I said at the beginning of this chapter that the relationship between a thing and the word that represents the thing was arbitrary, this is not actually absolutely true. There is a group of words which are an attempt to spell out a particular and specific sound. The words we have for animal noises are examples of this – 'buzz' to describe the sound a bee makes; 'moo' to represent a cow lowing; and 'cock-a-doodle-doo' for a cock crowing. There are places where this goes further and the sound becomes a thing-name in itself: quite a number of the names of British birds are based on the cries they make. The Green Plover is commonly called a 'peewit', not because we think it stupid but because these phonic signals approximate its distinctive cry. The curlews' calls have provided them with their name.

A number of quite ordinary words that we use for sounds – like bang, hiss, whisper, murmur, stutter and grunt – also seem to come into this category. The word sounds like the sound it represents, as opposed to, for example, the word 'sneeze', which does not sound anything at all like the high-force explosion of air that it represents.

More significantly for writers, sentences can do this too: they can sound like the thing you are describing – whether it is an object, an action or even an emotion. This kind of 'trick', attuned to the mental ear rather than the reading eye, can do a lot to make writing memorable and vivid. It reinforces the literal meaning of the words – rather like appropriate background music to a film. Look at this description:

> 'No one talks in these factories. Everyone is too busy. The only sounds are the snip, snip of scissors and the hum of sewing machines.'

The writer could have written the last sentence as, 'The only noises are of women cutting the cloth and the sewing machines working.' It is easy to see how much the repeated 'snip, snip' adds to the effect, and how the 'hum' sound is carried on to the 'm' at the beginning of the word 'machines'. But it is also worth noticing all those busy-sounding Ss – thirteen of them, five in a prominent position at the beginning of words – and how they make an energetic background noise.

The technical name for words that sound like the noises they represent is onomatopoeia. *The repetition of sounds within a piece of writing is called* assonance. *Assonance comes in various specific forms: for instance, the repetition of a consonant at the beginning of a word is* alliteration. *These sorts of linguistic effects are called* rhetorical devices. *There are lots and lots of them and they were first defined by the Greek classical writers, which is why they have such elaborate and usually unpronounceable names. If they interest you, you can find lists of them either through a web search under 'Rhetorical Devices' or in a book like*

Modern English Usage *by G. Fowler. In one sense the names do not matter, but it is useful to know them so that you can think about your own writing more consciously and powerfully. It is also fun to experiment with them in your own writing.*

Exercise 10 Describe sounds

☞ Take your notebook with you and go somewhere where there is a constant background noise – a beach, beside a waterfall, near a major road – and where you can sit quietly for a while. It is easier when you first work on this exercise not to try somewhere with a lot of human voices, like a children's playground.

☞ Sit and *listen*.

☞ Try to separate out and distinguish the various strands of sound – for example wind in trees and wind in telegraph wires make very different noises: together, with a number of other sound effects, they add up to the aural experience of a 'windy day'.

☞ Make careful notes of what you *can actually hear*. Try to eliminate any general sounds that you *expected* to hear – and include any surprising or unexpected ones that are genuinely audible. Add any interesting sights or smells or general 'feel' that enhance the sound.

☞ When you are next having a writing session – or immediately if possible – try to write a description of the experience that represents the soundscape – not intellectually but aurally. For example, not 'the sea sounded like a child telling a secret', but 'the waves whispered', assuming that is what you 'heard' them doing.

☞ Like the last exercises, you will probably need to 'fiddle about' with this bit of writing too. You will probably find, for example, that you want to read it aloud to check the sounds and then adjust what you have written to capture your experience more immediately. So this exercise will also introduce you to some more elementary editing skills – particularly the skill of listening to and looking at what you have got with real care.

☞ This is a game – you do not have to create great literature. You are just exploring one aspect of the words you are going to use to construct great literature.

THE ATMOSPHERE OF WORDS

As you get more confident with this way of using language, you may want to experiment with a more sophisticated version of this exercise. Instead of working directly with sounds, try taking the same sort of careful notes on different kinds of physical experience: waking up warm and comfortable in bed; being very cold and tired at the end of a long walk; dozing in the sunshine; being extremely excited about something that is about to happen (anticipation). Try and describe these sorts of situations in words that reinforce the sensations. The nineteenth-century poet, Alfred Tennyson, is particularly good at this. In his poem *The Lotus Eaters* he describes a group of sailors arriving on an island where they are lulled into a sort of drugged haze so that they lose all energy and motivation. He creates this atmosphere right from the opening verse of his poem:

In the afternoon they came unto a land
In which it seemed always afternoon.
All round the coast the languid air did swoon,
Breathing like one that hath a weary dream.
Full-faced above the valley stood the moon;
And like a downward smoke, the slender stream
Along the cliff to fall and pause and fall did seem.

Read this attentively. Try reading it aloud, and see if you can work out how Tennyson achieves this slow-moving dreamy effect as much by his choice of words as by anything he says explicitly.

Words tend to carry with them a sort of 'aura' or atmosphere. Different words feel more or less appropriate in different contexts, even when the meaning is completely clear. A bikini on a beach is entirely appropriate, but a bikini at a formal dinner, even if the room temperature is as high or higher than on the beach, is not appropriate; although an equally revealing and skimpy dress may well be perfect for the occasion. Words are like clothes in this sense – they don't just have a meaning function, they have an associated atmosphere too.

For example, my grown-up children call me 'Mummy' when they are speaking to me, but when they are speaking *about* me (even if I am there) they say 'my mother'. When they were little they did not make this distinction – most small children say 'my Mummy'. No one except my children ever calls me 'Mummy' (and I would think it very weird indeed if anyone did: nurses in the maternity unit used to do this, but mercifully they seem to have given it up now). The words 'mummy' and 'mother' have exactly the same meaning, but a very different register.

Words' effects

This is rather an elementary example, but I think it makes the point. The effect of this odd fact is that different words give a reader a different feeling, even when the explicit meaning is the same. The two words 'perambulate' and 'stroll' mean almost exactly the same sort of slightly idle walking, usually in a social or public context. We know they mean the same kind of movement, because the word for the wheeled vehicle that a baby is pushed about in is 'pram', a shortening of 'perambulator' in UK English, and a 'stroller' in US English. But they do not feel the same: 'perambulate' feels grander and more old-fashioned than 'stroll'; indeed in most contexts it now feels pretentious and affected.

Word processors

Even my word processor knows about linguistic register. Like most modern computers it has a 'spelling and grammar check' option. I can set the grammar check for a range of different contexts. Mine offers me four different language registers and will check in any of them – because what is acceptable and correct varies according to the register I tell it I plan to write in. As well as these four – casual, standard, formal and technical – it also allows me to set my own 'custom made' check, in case I want to write something that is none of those four.

I have a love affair with my word processor, which has speeded up my writing and made many of my professional duties so much easier and less irksome. Nonetheless I still say, 'Do not trust the spelling and grammar check.' Do not abrogate your own responsibility, or your own voice. The spelling check will not pick up a great range of basic spelling mistakes because the 'wrong spelling' is still a 'real word' as in their/there/they're. The grammar check will destroy your individual style with its nit-picking rules. Mine, for example, hates passive verb constructions. In the section before this one it kept wanting to change the passive sentence, 'There are lots and lots of them and they were first defined by the Greek classical writers,' *to the active form,* 'the Greek classical writers first defined these'. *In the context this makes no sense at all! I know passive sentences can be weak – but for a creative writer, they may sometimes be exactly what is needed in terms of the shape, sound and rhythm of the sentence.*

Language changes over time

These atmospheric associations of words are, like the words themselves, fairly arbitrary – they are based only on use and custom. We see that, very simply, in the way swear words change their insult-value over time. The list of words that the BBC will only broadcast 'after the watershed' (because they are judged to be offensive or unsuitable for children to hear) is constantly being argued about and renegotiated. Words that are slang one day become standard before too long; words that are original and lively become clichéd or pretentious from over-use or change of fashion.

Nonetheless this question of shade or tone is one of the most influential aspects of writing; and getting it wrong can do more to undermine the effectiveness of what we write than almost anything else. Unfortunately there is no right or wrong here – occasional shifts of register can be very effective or they can make a whole paragraph collapse. For the new writer the best you can do is try and become sensitive to what a word may be saying to the reader. You can develop this sensitivity by reading a lot, listening to other people talking in different situations, and by developing a sort of split personality, so that you can write without too much self-

The atmospheric associations of words are...based on use and custom

consciousness and then read back your own writing with your
antennae quivering with awareness.

But at least at the beginning of your writing journey one very good
way to sharpen up your sense of the various registers is by
experimenting with a variety of them.

Exercise 11 Experiment with atmosphere

☞ If you have been keeping up your scrapbook you may have,
ready to hand, the materials you need for this exercise. You
need a report from a local newspaper, which has a fairly
straightforward narrative. Something like a traffic accident or
minor crime is ideal. Read the journalist's account very
carefully, noticing both what happened and the language and
style that is used.

☞ Rewrite the story from a different point of view, in the first
person using 'I', not to describe your own personal reactions
but to create the voice of one of the characters in a very
particular context. For example – how would a child who saw
the events tell the story? How would a lawyer describe the
episode if he were defending one of the parties in front of a
judge? How might one of the people involved describe what
happened in the pub, or in a letter to his grandmother? Write
quite quickly, and try not to make it much longer than the
newspaper account.

☞ Now do it again – with different characters in different
contexts. Letters, formal reports, gossip.

☞ Try telling it in the third person in another context – how might a preacher incorporate the story as part of a sermon? How might an academic textbook relate the events? How might an official letter to someone involved sound?

☞ See if you can come up with six different versions of the story that show six different linguistic registers.

☞ Remember that this is a game – you do not have to create great literature. You are just exploring one aspect of the words you are going to use to construct great literature.

Part of this exercise is about what, in creative writing, is usually called 'point of view', an idea that we will come back to later. Point of view is a technical term and refers to questions about who is telling the story and what they could see and know. In this exercise I am trying to show you something slightly different. It is not really about the characters or the narrative; it is about the language itself. The same person would use a different language register in different situations – we all do it, almost without thinking or noticing.

I moved house last year and decided to send a single change of address note to everyone in my email address book. The body of the email was fine but when I came to the end I found signing-off rather difficult because I was forced to find a common register for people to whom I would normally use very different styles of closing an email. I did not want to say 'love and hugs, darling' to my bank manager, nor 'yours truly' to my son: both were in the wrong register. I took a look at past emails and found quite a large range, including:

> *Love from*
> *Warmly*

Best wishes

Yours

Yours sincerely

Warmest regards

(In the end I cheated. I signed the email, 'Sorry this is so brief, but you know what moving is like, Sara.' This seemed to be appropriate for almost all the contexts.) What I had was a problem of atmosphere – everything on the list says much the same thing, for much the same purpose, but in fact each conveys a very different message.

The reason why this matters so much in your writing is because you are trying to pull off a rather complicated juggling act.

Written versus spoken language

All written language has a slightly different register from spoken language – nearly everyone has a different vocabulary for writing and speaking. Most of us are not conscious of this. In English there are about 54,000 words (it depends how you count them) and an average literate adult, whose first language is English, can understand about 20,000 of them in print, but only uses about 3,000 when speaking. Your writing vocabulary almost certainly falls somewhere in between these two. Just to make it more complicated, people use different words to convey the same meaning when they are speaking or writing. For example, in spoken English, *let* is used four times more often than *allow*, but in written English, *allow* occurs nearly twice as often as *let*. *Permit* has a much more formal register than the others; it is fairly rare in speech and in writing turns up mainly in official documents.

However, in good creative writing you are very often trying to replicate (in writing) an authentic speaking voice, either directly in

English has the largest vocabulary of any language... 54,000 words

monologues and conversation, or less directly by giving a flavour of intimacy and reality to an emotional experience – by capturing the language of the experience as well as describing what is happening. Here the two registers will be in conflict if you are not very careful.

It is not easy to get this balance right. And the cost of getting it wrong is rather high: your reader will be jerked out of the mood you have worked so hard to get them into, and will recognize that the whole thing is a con trick. They will either get irritated and stop reading, or else, which is worse in many ways, get a fit of the giggles. Sudden and inappropriate shifts of register or atmosphere are very funny: this is often what lies behind the 'cute' sayings of small children, which make us grown-ups laugh. The best, perhaps the only, thing to do, is keep thinking about it:

- ❖ Be aware of it.
- ❖ Keep reading – look carefully at the way books you admire or enjoy handle this juggling act.
- ❖ Keep setting yourself writing exercises which explore this – writing, for example, monologues in the words of a child, or fictional letters in lawyers' formal register. (A friend of mine has a great game in which you have to describe things in the language-register of an estate agent's advertisement.)
- ❖ Keep on thinking about words and noticing what atmosphere they bring with them.

Your choice of vocabulary

In English there is nearly always a *choice*. English has the largest vocabulary of any language ever. Those 54,000 words are far more than any other language in the world gets to use. This is partly because there are so many 'Englishes' around the world: American and British English have mild differences compared with many African, Indian and Caribbean Englishes. It is horribly common for impertinent people to try and 'correct' those who use other Englishes, but these are fully developed Englishes of their own, and inevitably add to the size of the total English vocabulary. English also needs a big vocabulary to compensate for its primitive and inflexible grammar. Nonetheless the strengths and advantages of all these words are enormous too. There is practically no difference in literal meaning at all between 'let', 'allow' and 'permit'. You can choose the one that gives your sentence the register that you want it to have.

For those of you who are interested in writing poetry, a lot of people still believe that successful poetry needs a special register of its own – a kind of exclusive 'poetic' vocabulary full of weird ofts and o'ers and peculiar word orders. This is simply not true. The same 'rules' about register and atmosphere apply to contemporary poetry (even when it is using traditional forms and rhythms) as to prose.

THE RHYTHM OF WORDS

Rhythm is at the base of all art forms, and especially of writing. The anthropologists and historians all seem to agree that the first literature was words fitted to percussion – to drums and feet beating out rhythms. Before there was narrative or poetry or tunes there was dancing and drumming. Possibly the first thing a human being knows is the rhythm of its mother's heartbeat, in syncopation with the faster rhythm of its own foetal heart, and babies *in utero* soon appear to become aware of the rhythm of the mother's day.

Rhythm affects mood and pace and our relationships with those around us. Songs and poetry stick more easily and firmly in our memories than chunks of prose do. Those mythologies which tell us that the world was brought into existence by the gods drumming, or by the slow rhythmic beating of a great bird's wings – pulling up the hills and pushing down the valleys – were onto a profound if dimly realized truth. In the beginning was rhythm.

All spoken language inevitably has a rhythm because we can only speak when we are breathing out. Although, when compared to other mammals, we have a great deal of voluntary control over how fast we breathe out, which allows us to vary the length and volume of sentences, there are physiological limits on this which impose, however subtly, a definite rhythm and pace on spoken language. Written language, however, does not naturally have these constraints. There is no reason, technically, why you should not write a totally arhythmic sentence that is five or six pages long. But you are unlikely to want to because such a sentence will not convey much emotional or dynamic meaning to your readers. Interestingly, before people learned to read silently in the third century CE there were no punctuation marks on written texts – reading aloud imposed a shape and rhythm on the sentence. Punctuation marks were principally invented to replace this breathing rhythm and help the silent reader to follow the sentence structure. Almost any grammatically written sentence will have some rhythm to it and that rhythm will affect any response to the sentence, almost without the reader being aware of it.

How often have you been reading something and found yourself falling asleep willy-nilly or being completely unable to concentrate? Sometimes this is because the subject matter is excruciatingly boring, but normally we do not set out to read books about things that we find boring; or, if we started in error, we just stop. Much more often it is because the *writing* is boring – and the most common sort of boring writing is writing without a sufficiently stimulating rhythm; or where the rhythm and pace do not match the subject matter emotionally.

...the first literature was words fitted to percussion — to drums and feet beating out rhythms

We do not like, on the whole, to be asked to gallop through complex emotional scenes, nor to dawdle through chase scenes – we need the rhythm to 'match' the thing we are reading about, and it is capturing this skill that will improve the quality of your writing enormously.

Rhythm in poetry

Rhythm, like sound and shape and register, is under the control of the writer. This applies as much to prose as it does to poetry, but it is much easier to analyse rhythm in poetry. We all know what we mean when we say, 'it doesn't scan'. But rhythm is not just a set of hoops, which poets have to show they can jump through – it is fundamentally important to the mood and atmosphere and therefore the total meaning of the poem.

To take a very simple example, look at the following short passages, and read them aloud if you need to:

O, young Lochinvar is come out of the West
Through all the wide border his steed was the best;
And save his good broadsword he weapons had none,
He rode all unarmed, and he rode all alone.

Sir Walter Scott

Faster than fairies, faster than witches,
Bridges and houses, hedges and ditches. . .
Here is a child who clambers and scrambles
All by himself and gathering brambles.

Robert Louis Stevenson

It is easy enough to see that the first is a poem about someone making a fast journey on horseback, and the second is about a person looking out of a (steam) train window. In both cases the poets have chosen and worked on a language rhythm that imitates the rhythm of the movement they are describing. You can also see that to make it work both poets have had to make compromises. Scott has distorted the natural grammatical word order of the sentence (this is most obvious in line three) and Stevenson has had to tuck in a rather excessive number of *ands* to get the very lightly stressed syllables he needs. Both Scott and Stevenson were experienced poets – here they both judged that the rhythmic effect was worth the compromise. They may well have made the decision based on other criteria as well: Scott's poem is set in the mediaeval period so he may have thought that the rather archaic sentence structure was less of a problem; and Stevenson was writing for children, who love poetry technique and games with rhythm, possibly because they are still enchanted by what language might be able to do.

Rhythm in prose

Rhythm is less blatant in prose but it is just as important. In the following passage, from *Emma* by Jane Austen, you can see how the writer captures the idle thoughts and increasing exhaustion of Mrs. Elton who is picking strawberries, by arranging her phrases with the rhythm of human breath:

'...The best fruit in England – every body's favourite – always wholesome. – These the finest beds and finest sorts. – Delightful to gather for one's self – the only way of really enjoying them. – Morning decidedly the best time – never tired – every sort good – delicious fruit – only too rich to be eaten much of – inferior to cherries – currants more refreshing – only objection to gathering strawberries the stooping – glaring sun – tired to death – could bear it no longer – must go and sit in the shade.'

In these three pieces, the rhythm directly replicates and enhances the background meaning of the words. Usually the function of rhythm is rather more subtle than this and less explicit in its intention. Often the rhythm of a sentence or paragraph is not so much to emphasize the meaning in this direct way as to increase the reader's pleasure, and therefore the power and influence that the writing has over them. As I have already mentioned, this may be as basic as keeping them awake and paying attention! However, rhythm can do more complex things than that – above all it can set a kind of tone or mood. We all know this from the effect that different dance rhythms induce in us: waltz music makes you *feel* very differently when compared to the feelings brought about by a Scottish reel tune; the tempo of a polka makes you feel very differently to the insistent pulse of modern dance music.

Reading out loud

The best exercise for newer writers in this particular skill is *reading aloud*. If (like most people) you do not happen to live in a household where this is a common practice you may find it awkward when you begin – a kind of crippling self-consciousness overcomes people and they find themselves bundling through at top speed just to get the job over, or they shirk it altogether. I believe that developing the ability to read one's own work aloud, to oneself or others, and hear it properly, is one of the best ways of developing a strong and authentic voice, an individual and rich style. It is a great editing tool, and I will be coming back to this. It is extraordinary how even very simple typing errors, such as words left out, can hide themselves from your editorial eye, but become glaringly apparent to your editorial ear. You will also find that you can notice much more quickly and accurately any sentences where the grammar or individual choice of word is not quite right. The sound and the register of your writing will come into an immediate and sharp focus; and pace and rhythm will expose their dynamic in a fresh and often exciting way. I cannot urge you too strongly to try and develop this habit.

Exercise 12 Reading aloud

☞ Find a quiet place where you will not be interrupted or overheard.

☞ Pretend you are in public. Stand up. Imagine a listener a few feet away from you: you are reading to and for this person at all times. You don't need to shout but you do need to speak slowly and clearly enough for that listener to understand.

☞ Start with something that is not by you, but that you really enjoy reading. If you already have a sense that a piece of writing has a rich rhythmic aspect then that is a good piece to work with. I would recommend starting with poetry – and particularly with blank verse.

Blank verse is non-rhyming poetry, often written in a verse form called iambic *pentameter, which has five stressed syllables to each line:* di-dum, di-dum, di-dum, di-dum, di-dum.

> *If MU-sic BE the FOOD of LOVE, play ON*
> *Give ME ex-CESS of IT that SUR-feit-ING*
> *The AP-pe-TITE may SICK-en AND so DIE.*

This is the verse form of many Elizabethan dramatists, of Milton's epic poems and of Wordsworth's The Prelude. *It is a very good starting point for rhythmical reading because a great deal of variation within the strict form is possible. You will see, for example, that in these three lines from Shakespeare's* Twelfth Night *there is a natural pause in each line – but it is in a different place each time (after LOVE in l.1; after IT in l.2 and after SICK-en in l.3) This makes it rhythmically – and therefore emotionally – very flexible.*

☛ If you prefer contemporary work – Seamus Heaney's translation of *Beowulf* or Carol Anne Duffy's 'The Laughter of Stafford Girls' High' in *Feminine Gospels*, to name just two examples among many, would be excellent. If poetry makes you feel too much as though you were back in school there are plenty of non-poetry passages you can use for this too – most obviously the Authorised translation of the Bible, which is famous for its rhythmic prose; try the Book of Isaiah. But any writer whose work you enjoy and who is rhythmically rich is worth exploring.

☛ Listen to what you are reading. Play around with it. Read it in a di-dum, di-dum way, and then read it emotionally. Experiment with reading against the rhythm, or completely flat. Get inside not so much the meaning of the writing but the texture and feel and the very words of it.

☛ Now read one of the exercises you did from the first chapter of this book. Try and treat it in exactly the same way. Listen to what you have written carefully and respectfully.

☛ If you find the whole business completely cringe-making, try finding a child to read to. They will appreciate your efforts. Luckily there is a lot of good poetry for children around now

– and many prose writers have realised how much quite small children enjoy rhythm. *The Man Whose Mother was a Pirate* by Margaret Mahy is a technical masterpiece, a delightful story, linguistically rich and could be used as a textbook for almost all the ideas in this chapter.

If you want to pursue the concept of rhythm then a very good exercise is to try and write poems using traditional forms – ballads, sonnets, blank verse, even limericks. The quickest way to establish the structural and rhythmic challenges for each of these, and other, forms is to look on the Internet. Try searching under 'poetic forms' if you want some new ideas, or 'poetic form' + 'sonnet', for example, if you know specifically what you want to know more about. If you come to find this sort of writing exciting you will probably want to own a dictionary of poetic form, and some specialist poetry course books. I have made some suggestions in the bibliography on p. 236.

It is always worth remembering that as well as rhythm within a sentence or paragraph there is also the larger underlying rhythm of a whole work – be it a longer poem, story, play, novel or memoir – just as there is rhythm within each bar and passage of a symphony and also a rhythmic relationship between the movements and in the overall effect of the whole piece. I tend to think of the overall large-scale rhythm of a book as 'pace' and keep the word 'rhythm' to describe a language pattern which may only be a few words long.

...as well as rhythm within a sentence or paragraph there is also the larger underlying rhythm of a whole work

THE HISTORY OF WORDS

In one sense the history of words is less obviously central to a writer's immediate concerns than the other items on my list. You might feel, for example, that since everyone knows what 'spinster' means *now*, then why should the writer care that it originally meant an *independent woman capable of earning her own living* (through spinning, one of the few profitable trades open to women); not a woman who didn't or couldn't get married, but a woman who did not need to get married. It was later extended to all unmarried women as a compliment to the ones who weren't good spinners – so that their marriages could be seen as free choices rather than driven by dire economic necessity.

Nonetheless I do believe that it is important that writers keep an eye on the way words have developed because *they are still developing* – look at 'wicked' for example. In street language it means the exact opposite of what it once meant and this is in fact a second big change for this poor word: originally it meant 'miserable' and comes from the same root as wretched. Each time you use a word in a piece of creative writing, you are pushing on its boundaries of meaning – you have put it into a brand new context. If you bounce it too far away from its roots people will not understand you, but if you do not develop it at all your writing will sound clichéd.

Etymology is the history of individual words; their roots and how the words change over the years. English is a very interesting language, etymologically, because it has been created from so many different sources. Modern English developed from Anglo-Saxon, a language brought to Britain by Scandinavian and German invaders: essentially it is a Teutonic language, so we share the roots of a great many words with modern German. Then in 1066 the Norman invaders imposed a thick layer of French on the indigenous language. French is a Romance Language drawing on the same sources as Italian and Spanish, for example, and all of them derived from Latin.

One result of this admixture affects 'register.' Because French, and later French-influenced English, was the language of the ruling classes, words with a French origin usually have a 'higher' or grander

It is important that writers keep an eye on the way words have developed because they are still developing

register than their Anglo-Saxon parallels. So we call our central institution of government 'Parliament' (a French word from '*parler*' to talk.) But before the Norman Conquest the similar political gatherings were called 'moots': an Anglo-Saxon word, which also gives us the verb 'to meet' and the noun 'meeting'. An ordinary 'meeting' is not as important as a parliament. Interestingly, the word 'moot' still lives on in expressions like 'a moot point' – an arguable or debateable issue.

A really good example of this is the way English, unlike other European languages, has a different word for farm animals when they are alive and when they are being eaten. The poor agricultural workers, who seldom got to eat meat, kept the Anglo-Saxon words, but the rich who had little to do with animals but a lot more to do with their meat used French words. So we have:

Anglo-Saxon: cow. French: *boeuf*. English cow-meat: beef
Anglo-Saxon: sheep. French: *mouton*. English sheep-meat: mutton
Anglo Saxon: pig. French: *porc*. English pig-meat: pork
Anglo-Saxon: calf. French: *veau*. English calf-meat: veal

If you want to be of the plain spoken 'call a spade a spade' school of writing you should keep a sharp eye out for Anglo-Saxon words which tend to be shorter, blunter and less 'fancy'. If you want to heighten your register, then look for a more French-based vocabulary.

To complicate the matter further Latin itself remained the language of the Church, and therefore of education, long enough to influence English directly. Latin inevitably brought with it a whole set of Greek words, especially in areas like science and abstract thinking. In later times Britain's overseas expansion added a whole new range of words to British English – and led to the development of other Englishes, including of course American English, each with their own particular vocabularies. A curious example – in Eastern Africa the word 'late' can mean 'dead', as in 'my parents are both late, I am an orphan'. This is not a coy euphemism; it derives from the old-fashioned way of describing a dead person as 'the late Mr. Smith.'

An understanding of etymology and the way it affects tone and style and subtle gradations of meanings seems to me one of the more interesting ways a writer can influence the reader's imagination, and give depth and subtlety of meaning and resonance. The selection of vocabulary along these lines is also a powerful way of locating characters in their geographical place without having to go to the contortions of representing regional accents. Above all, getting into the bones of language, excavating its layers and claiming it as your own, is like any good worker taking care of and respecting their tools. The more you understand how something works, the more easily and efficiently you can use it.

So here is a little exercise to get you started:

Exercise 13 Read what you have written

- ☞ You need to find a dictionary big enough to have at least some basic etymology in it. If you do not own one yourself, every library in the country does.

- ☞ Look up the following words (they all have some odd quirk of history): *gossip, adultery, kangaroo, music, television, orange, sandwich, marathon, husband, lunatic.*

- ☞ Since you have got the dictionary out, look up ten other words that you have recently used in your notebook or other writing.

- ☞ Write a few sentences, or even, if you are enjoying yourself, a little story that reveals something about the origin and roots of some of these words while still using them in a modern sense.

As well as making you think about etymology I hope this exercise will also help you to feel *playful* about language. You should make a hobby and a habit of playing about in the dictionary. I am not suggesting that you try and insert obscure or pedantic words into your writing, but rather that you realize just how peculiar and delightful the whole business of language really is.

Chapter 3 What you

In a sense the last two chapters are it – that is all you need to start and continue what will be, I hope, a life-long and enriching pastime that will be personally rewarding. To sum up, therefore, you need:

❖ A way of generating raw materials, of finding out what happens when you sit down and write, plus an inner confidence that this is worth doing.

❖ A basic awareness that language itself is a complicated tool-of-your-trade. Like all precision instruments it needs technical understanding, careful handling and regular maintenance.

Assuming that you have applied yourself to the exercises, and experimented with at least a good number of them – and you have started to develop a writing habit – then you are writing. You are a writer.

Everything else in this book is not going to be about how to write, but about how to write *better*.

In preparation for this move forward, you now need to do what I tried to stop you from doing when you first did the exercises in the *Travelling the way* chapter. You need to read what you have written, critically and intelligently.

Exercise 14 How to read your own writing
☞ If you do not already own some highlighter pens, go and buy at least three in different colours. For the purposes of this exercise we'll say they are pink, green and orange. If you are putting your exercises directly onto your word processor and do not know how the highlighter works – find out.

might write

➪ Read everything you have written since you started. Read slowly and carefully, from beginning to end, including all the exercises, everything in your notebook, everything in your journal if you are keeping one, any notes you took on the exercises and anything else you may have written outside the exercises I suggested. Read it all through; try and enjoy it. Even if it seems weak or not what you hoped it would be, you can at least appreciate the fact that you have accomplished something. Admire yourself. Laugh at your jokes if you made any, and be willing to be moved by your own emotions, proud of your own observations and delighted at the number of pages you have covered.

➪ Put it all away again, overnight if possible. If you will not be able to have another decent writing session for a few days, take a break of at least fifteen minutes instead, and then come back to it.

➪ Read it all again.

➪ This time, as you read, highlight in pink anything you like or find interesting, for whatever reason. *(No one except you is ever going to see this – you will gain nothing if you start worrying that you are too boastful, showing off, shallow, morbid or useless.)* When you are highlighting in this way you are not claiming that you are a genius or that the words you are marking so cheerfully are Immortal Art – you are just drawing to your own personal attention something that you like or find interesting.

☞ In green, highlight anything in your *Travelling the way* exercises that you can see relates to the Language exercises – where you have used shape, or sound, or rhythm in the writing; where you recognize that you have selected a word in the right or wrong 'register'. Anything at all where you are using language interestingly. Also in green, highlight anything in the Language exercises where you can see you have gone beyond the purely technical aspects of the exercise and started to write something that has real meaning for you – anything that relates to the *Travelling the way* chapter.

☞ In orange, highlight anything that you now want to change.

☞ If you are anything like me, you probably need to jot down in your notebook which colour you used for what.

☞ Read again through all the coloured passages.

☞ Write for at least ten minutes about this experience of reading your own writing.

It is quite important that while doing this exercise you try not to look at each piece as a whole (unless they are very short indeed). While I was describing the exercises in the previous chapters I stressed that these exercises are not attempts at creating 'great literature', but simply a way to generate the raw materials of your own future writing. If you did actually do this exercise with integrity and without too much going back and correcting, changing and adjusting, it is highly unlikely that anything you have written for it will be a beautiful, balanced whole.

Even if you do think that some piece is exquisitely wonderful, that is not what should interest you most at this point. What we are looking for here are the nuggets or diamonds in the piles of ore and rubble you have dug up in your searching.

What you will most probably find is that there is a reasonable amount of pink, a smaller amount of green (subject matter usually comes before technique although this is not inevitably the case) and most of all of orange. The most exciting thing to find is a passage that needed all three colours. If the inner material that you created almost spontaneously **and** a sense that the language you have expressed it in is rich in one way or another **and** a desire to work on it and make it better all come together then something truly creative is happening – no wonder it looks a bit confused.

If your coloured pages look very different from this arrangement, there are various things that might be happening.

If you have no, or very few – say less than two per cent – pink phrases or sentences then consider the following:

❖ Your inner censor is being unnecessarily savage. You could try again, deliberately being kinder to yourself and more alert to your own writing. Or you could ask a friend to do the exercise for you (only the pink part).

❖ You could try again using a different guidebook. (There are so many techniques and approaches for gathering your raw material that an obvious thought is that this is not the right book for you.)

❖ You could give up altogether, or try a different art form. But this option seems a bit foolish or cowardly if you have got as far as this.

If you have a great deal of pink – say over eighty per cent – and especially if you also have very little of the third colour then possibly one of the following is the case:

❖ You are a natural genius. You do not need this, or any other map. You only need to get on with it. Out of curiosity you might ask yourself why you have not previously discovered how brilliant you are.

❖ Your inner critic is being a bit over-indulgent. You could try taking a week off writing and read a lot of really successful or (better still) great writing.

❖ You have dug up some raw material that has shown you something really important about yourself. This is exciting and very promising, but you may need to think more about the reader's needs if you are serious about the writing.

If you have a very high proportion of green, or a disproportionate amount of pink appears in the Language exercises (rather than the *Travelling the way* exercises) something really interesting is going on. There are a number of possibilities:

❖ You have an enviably good ear for written language, but have not yet discovered your own unique voice. Try some more exercises from the first section – writing faster and with less conscious control.

❖ You are well read and perhaps slightly over-awed by the technical accomplishments of writers whom you admire.

❖ You are primarily a poet, rather than a storyteller. The best advice may be simple: read lots and lots of contemporary poetry. (Of course you should also do this if you have no green marks in the opening exercises or no pink marks in the second set of exercises.)

I am aware that there is a danger of this turning into one of those magazine quizzes that attempt to define your 'personality type' by a series of multiple-choice questions. I don't think that writers really fall into particular categories in any simple sense. Most of us come to the task with at least a sense of what we might want to do with the writing as well as a desire to write. The intention behind this exercise is to help you to look at and think about your own writing positively and usefully.

I have said all along that these exercises are nothing more than ways of getting into writing. If you find them interesting, supportive or joyful then there is a good case for pushing on with this sort of experimental exercise for a bit longer, possibly forever, even if you become very successful in one particular form or another. I am, at the moment, in my mid-fifties and really regretting that I have never developed a poetry voice, because I was so sure I knew what I was doing and it looked like 'prose' to me. You will almost certainly find that something emerges from the task, and in the meanwhile you will be developing technically and nothing that you do will be wasted. A great many writers do in fact write in all sorts of forms and genres – even if they only publish in one or two of them: the curiosity about writing itself should spread and move forward like a river.

Where to next?

When people begin to write, or begin to take an impulse to write

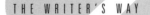

more seriously, they obviously cannot know much about their own writing. So they cannot really have much idea about what they might be capable of. Looking at what you make out of this sort of ongoing writing practice is part of developing an understanding of where you might go next.

Another way of thinking about 'where you might go next' is to look at some possible destinations.

Often, when I plan a holiday, I start with a very vague, semi-instinctual idea: 'I would like to go to Africa' or 'I would like to visit some mountains'. This is followed by a kind of research period, which is mainly practical: How do I get to Africa? What exactly do I want to see and do when I get there? What is there to see and do when I get there? Then, as I learn more, I develop my plan in more detail: what might I like to see? Can I go to both A and B in the time/for the money I have got? Shall I pre-book a hotel or take a chance on finding somewhere?

I hope that something a bit like that is going on for you now. You have a broad general idea: 'I would like to be writing.' In the exercises we have looked at so far we have been researching this very broad idea. Now is the time to go and buy a specific guidebook – what are the possible destinations in this land-of-writing?

So I am now going to take a very brief conducted tour of some of the major landmarks of that country. This is a writer's guide, not a reader's guide; and it includes, at this point, only the briefest tourist notes. Remember you are still only thinking about what you might write – you can fantasize, dream, aspire to and take notes towards more than one journey at the same time.

An additional point: this chapter is about writing for its own sake; it is not about professional or commercial opportunities. Towards the end of this book I will offer some suggestions about ways to move towards publication and financial reward (such as it is), but this is more a literary tour than career advice.

What is creative writing?

The first question, of course, has to be what **is** creative writing? Where do its boundaries lie? For example, good advertising slogans are wonderful works of language, imagery, economy and rhetorical devices. Good TV ads are compact dramas full of dynamism, wit and character observation. Moreover, all advertising has an underlying meaning and deploys symbols, cultural forms and imaginative psychology. To suggest that copywriters are not creative writers would be silly; and yet, when you picked up this book, I bet you did not anticipate that it would contain advice on how to write good advertising copy. The same might be said about many non-fiction books: they may be creatively conceived, beautifully written and give enormous reading pleasure, but a critical work on the sonnets of Wordsworth or a history of the Second World War are not what we mean when we talk about 'creative writing' or 'literature'. But then, oddly, we would also feel that some non-fiction books were very definitely 'creative writing' – autobiography is often, though not always, something other than a 'history'. Memoirs, musings and certain imaginative books of philosophy or spirituality, for example, fit quite comfortably into our minds as 'creative writing'.

I used to think that the division was about the writer's *intentions*. If they intended the work to be a communication of something about themselves, to other people, using words, then it was creative writing – but as soon as they had another intention, like educating, instructing, explaining something outside themselves, or persuading the reader about intellectual or abstract ideas (to buy a particular

...you can fantasize, dream, aspire to and take notes towards more than one journey at a time brand of anything, whether of soap powder or ideology) then it fell outside the boundaries of 'pure' literature. However, I now think that is not quite right – many great novels and poems, clearly right in the centre of the creative writing tradition, have very strong educational or ideological motives. In fact very few major works of literature do not have some strong intellectual or psychological point of view that they quite consciously want to convey to their readers. One could draw a line perhaps by suggesting that 'creative writing' asks questions of the reader's imagination – 'What if. . . ?' – whereas other forms of writing make a statement to the reader's intellect – 'It is the case that. . .' But even this breaks down quite quickly in the face of all the exceptions.

You could say that creative writing is any work that must be read as a whole to get its fullest meaning. Novels do not have indexes – you can't look up the bit you want to know and leave the rest unread.

You could say, as Plato more or less said, that creative writing means writing that tells lies – or at least is writing where it does not matter if the writer does not tell the logical and consistent truth.

You could say that creative writing begins at the point where the writer's 'I' – whether as character or as narrator – is the central point of the exercise.

You could say that creative writing was any writing that, first and foremost, told a story.

All these things are a bit true but not entirely, or perhaps they are all true at the same time.

So I have now come to the conclusion that it is well-nigh impossible to come up with a clear and workable definition; and yet at the same time I think everyone feels that there is a distinction. Perhaps we all put our boundaries in slightly different places. So if you feel that I have included or excluded anything in what follows

...the skills of creative writing will unquestionably help you make any sort of writing you do more readable

that does not quite fit for you, then you may very well be right. And in a sense it does not matter very much – because, especially along that ill-defined border, the skills of creative writing will unquestionably help you make *any* sort of writing you do more readable, more emotionally meaningful and more satisfying both for the reader and for you, the writer. Even if my definition is not quite yours, or you know that what you want to write does not quite fall into a category that you feel comfortable calling creative writing, you can still use this book and learn valuable techniques from it.

So, with all these excuses and doubts in place, I think we can simply say that there are two main sections of creative writing – prose and poetry.

Poetry

Defining poetry in the early twenty-first century is a bit of a nightmare. T.S. Eliot did quite well with his suggestion that poetry was 'writing with a lot of white space around the words'. Although this can look pretty trite I think it is revealing. In poetry the words have a particular and heightened importance – poems are language constructions in a very direct way that prose is not. All the things I was writing about in the last chapter – the sound and space and register and rhythm of language – are foregrounded in poetry. This, of course, is why so many of my examples in the last chapter came from poems – you can isolate and look at them there, much more easily than you can in prose.

Above all perhaps the whole idea of metaphor is absolutely central to poetry. It is vital in prose as well – indeed in all human language and expression – but in poetry the idea that a word (or phrase or sentence) can carry both its own literal meaning, and – when properly organized into the poem by the poet – a whole other set of meanings as well, has a special and primary importance.

Metaphor, at one level is simply one more rhetorical device. Metaphor compares two different things by speaking of one in terms of the other. Unlike a simile or analogy, which provide us with a way of saying that one thing is like another – 'She looked like an angel' – a metaphor asserts that one thing is another thing, 'You are an angel'. Here is an example from the writing of Joshua Reynolds, an eighteenth-century painter and thinker:

> *'The mind is but a barren soil; a soil which is soon exhausted and will produce no crop, or only one, unless it be continually fertilized and enriched with foreign matter.'*

(Metaphor is so key to the whole activity of creative writing that I am going to be exploring it in more detail later. But if the idea intrigues you, you could read it now on p.110)

For these sorts of reasons, poetry imposes a particular rigour on the writer. There is a craft discipline and a learning process that runs along tightly entwined in the other process of personal growth, experience and thought. If, as you move through the exercises and ideas in this book you feel a growing desire to write poetry, or if indeed you came to the practice of creative writing because you already knew that you wanted to write poetry, then at the very least you should be immersing yourself in other people's poetry. Unless you are a very experienced reader you should probably invest in a specialist course book.

To be honest, I am not a poet and yet I still think that the writing of poetry represents the most complete or 'highest' form of everything I believe about creative writing. I do not exactly envy poets because they have a very difficult time – but I do yearn.

Prose

In a sense 'prose' is simply everything else.

However it is worth breaking down a little further into several specific forms. This is so you may be able to think about where you might go next, what you might like to work on.

There are three basic categories of prose writing; and all of them can be further divided into sub-categories:

- ❖ Fiction
- ❖ Drama
- ❖ Non-fiction

FICTION

Essentially fiction is the inventing of stories, which are written to be read (rather than heard or seen). Even when they are made up of real events, people or memories, they are still not claiming to be 'true' in the way a newspaper story is supposed to be true.

Novels

The most common form of prose fiction, from the reader's point of view, is the novel. A novel is a made-up story, of considerable length – nowadays usually between 70,000 and 120,000 words long.

We could add to this a little perhaps – a novel is a story *about people*. (In some novels the people are lightly disguised as aliens or animals – but it is always more of a fancy dress than a serious attempt to deceive the reader.) A novel, in this sense, is a story that is dependent on certain other sets of ideas – the most important one is that individuals are different from each other, and have some control over their own lives. The novel emerged with the emergence of ideas about individuality and personal freedom: it is closely linked to that development in thinking. A novel is a story about people and is governed by the concept of *psychology*. A novel with no individual psychological elements would not be a novel: it would simply be a story.

As you might guess from the word 'novel', which means 'new', this is the youngest form of literature we have. It is also presently the most popular in terms of readership and is what people usually think of first when they think about fiction.

Genre novels

Some critics want to break the novel down further, and talk about *genre* novels.

Genre *is a literary critical word meaning the particular type of something. (It has the same origin as words like genetic, or genus in plants and animals.) Usually it is a collective term for any adjective that could be applied to a novel in order to make it clearer what the reader might expect: detective novel, historical novel, science fiction novel, fantasy novel, pornographic novel and so on.*

In this context *genre* is too often used in a sneering kind of way. The implication is that there are 'real' novels and then inferior, less classy items called *genre novels*. But this is a nonsensical sort of snobbery in my opinion. It is nonsensical in both directions actually. On the one hand, *literary* novels and *middlebrow* novels are as governed by their own rules and expectation as any Western or thriller novel. (*Literary* is just as much an adjective as *detective* in this context.) On the other, it is very much a matter of fashion as to what is considered a *literary* and what is considered a *genre* novel. *Frankenstein* by Mary Shelley and *1984* by George Orwell are both 'sci-fi' novels. *A Tale of Two Cities* by Charles Dickens and *Middlemarch* by George Eliot are both historical novels. *The Scarlet*

Letter is pure Gothic fantasy and *All Quiet on the Western Front* is hard-core war genre. Jane Austen wrote the chick-lit of her day.

Do not be afraid of the label *genre novel*: if it is what you like to read there is a good chance that you will enjoy writing it. Whether or not it turns into a good novel is an entirely different question.

Short stories

The other major form of prose fiction is the short story.

When it comes to definitions the short story is a shy and timorous little beast – and every time you try and pin it down it slips away into the forest or changes shape almost magically.

A short story is a piece of prose writing, probably longer than 300 words, and probably shorter than 10,000 (though there are exceptions at both ends of this). It shares with poetry an intensification of language and structure, and it shares with novels a strong element of 'human interest'. It can be closer to poetry – in that it is principally concerned with an idea or metaphor; or it can be closer to the novel – in that it is principally concerned with the connection between character and event.

The short story used to be a very successful medium, independent and resilient. At present it has been through a period of massive decline – mostly because of the collapse of serious periodical publishing (although BBC Radio 4 alone commissions over 250 new short stories a year) and is too often treated as a sort of 'training ground' for future novelists. But I believe a short story is to a novel what a photograph is to a film. A good photograph is not a cinema short – it is a completely different thing of its own. We do not expect all photographers to 'grow up' and become film directors.

In another sense though short stories are quite a good form for writers to start with because there are surprisingly few rules, so you can try out anything you want; and because the length of time between the first draft and the editing process is shorter – which makes it good practice. It is possible to have a 'whole work' sooner, and this means you can think about editing and form and structure and balance and pace and rhythm earlier.

I am a short story writer. I think it is a wonderful, infinitely engaging and openhearted form of writing and reading. I think a good short story, more than the novel, allows writers to develop a unique voice and communicate through it. It gives the reader an experience unlike any other. The writing and publishing of short stories is one of the marks of a vibrant literary culture. I admit I am biased.

There are other forms of fiction writing as well:

The novella is a work of fiction that is not long enough to be a novel but which does not 'feel' like a long short story; it is usually about 20,000–30,000 words long. This is a form that attracts a great many writers, but has never really proven very popular with readers.

The novelette tends to be a rude or sneering word for a short, usually romantic, novel.

Writing for children is a specialised form of storytelling, often incorporating design or graphic elements into the text. Children's fiction tends to be shorter than adult fiction and needs to develop a very high level of identification between the reader and the principal character or characters. It is also a territory for wilder flights of the imagination and a certain anarchic flamboyance.

If you feel a desire to write for children, after you have finished working through this book you will almost certainly need to consult an expert. I have suggested some book titles and web pages in the bibliography.

Young adult fiction, which in its turn blends almost seamlessly into the standard novel.

Probably the best advice here is to write the book you want to write and see who wants to read it afterwards.

DRAMA

For the moment I am lumping plays, radio plays, TV and film scripts – and probably a number of other things as well – into this single section. Drama is simply a particular and specific kind of fiction. From the writer's point of view the main difference between the other forms of prose fiction and drama is that drama puts another level of distance or interpretation – the performance, including the actors, director and technicians – between the writer and the reader.

Some writers like that idea and others do not. Think about yourself in this context.

The particular skills of writing drama are obviously a seriously good ear for dialogue and, less obviously, a strong sense of structure. Drama is radically different from other prose fiction because we can only know about the characters those things that they are capable of saying and doing. Their inner secret life must, by and large, remain hidden. In this sense dramatic characters are more like 'real' people than the characters in novels are. We cannot go inside the heads of either characters in drama or real people, but we can go into the secret lives of characters in prose fiction.

On the other hand drama can evoke and present a particular range of emotions because the actors are always real. Drama is the most ancient form of literature, and it represents community and cooperation in a way that the novel cannot.

NON-FICTION

As I mentioned at the beginning of this section it is not easy to say where the line between 'creative non-fiction' and other sorts of writing actually falls. But I know that the initial impulse to think about writing at all can frequently arise from a need to tell a personal story, a story for which you, the writer, want to make a clear truth claim. The desire to tell the truth can get in the way of the story – because life is not usually structured like a good plot. In one sense this sort of story needs to be treated, from the writing point of view, as though it were a novel. Where that is the case I think it is creative writing.

At the moment we are in a phase of our cultural history where fiction, particularly novels, is failing its readers (or perhaps the readers are failing the fiction). People seem to have the greatest difficulty in identifying with fictional stories – of getting a personal truth out of something they know has been 'made-up'. This has led to a massive expansion in what I am calling 'creative non-fiction' – the very words 'true story' seem to give a book a kind of authority. The word 'confessional' has changed meaning – it now principally means something quite different from 'admitting your sins or failings', and has come to mean something more like 'revealing a secret', with a strong emphasis on the sympathetic, rather than the weak or even wicked, activities of the narrator. Such accounts have great attraction to many of us as readers, and it is a very tempting form of writing. Nonetheless the most exciting or harrowing or touching story still needs to be written well. Think about the pub

It is always a useful discipline to ask yourself every now and then 'What sort of writing have I created?'

bore – no matter how potentially interesting the events he labours over are, his clumsy rendering of them quickly reduces them to the tedious. The good storyteller, though, can make hilarious or interesting tales out of more or less nothing at all.

It's your choice

So here you are confronted with all these choices. Even if you have a strong sense of what you want to write it is worth thinking through the whole question again at this point. Whatever you decide to do next will – or at least should – fill up many hours of the next period of your life. It is worth being as clear as possible before you commit yourself. I suggest that you think again about *why* you started wanting to write and try and remember and imagine what you thought you would be doing with the writing.

As you begin the difficult struggle with the actual techniques of writing well, it can be helpful too, to have some idea of where you might like to be *going*. Of course you can change your mind – and in many ways I very much hope that you will, at least once, and perhaps several times. It is always a useful discipline to ask yourself every now and again, 'What sort of writing have I actually got here, what sort of writing have I created?' This question requires you to find a balance between aspiration and the concrete reality of what you have put on the page. It is a much more useful question than 'what sort of a writer do I want to be?', which can lead to nothing more than daydreams.

The exercises in this book are included for this very reason – to make you *think* about your writing. They aren't called 'exercises' for nothing – they are like a writing gym. They are meant, gradually and progressively, to get you fit. But like physical gym exercises, it is a great deal easier if you have some idea of what you want to be fit for – weightlifting and childbirth really do require different sets of exercises.

I keep an ongoing reading list at the back of my notebook, so that I can look at my reading separately from my writing over quite a long period of time. This is probably one of the best mental gym exercises you can do. I try, not always entirely successfully, to keep notes that link up my reading to my own writing.

Exercise 15 Make a reading list

➥ In your notebook make a list of everything you can remember reading in the last month. (You can leave out 'sell by dates' on yoghurt pots in your fridge. Try and include everything else.)

➥ Underline all the books (plus other creative writing – like stories or poems in magazines or letters and emails from friends that were attempts to write about something personal and real to them) and add any films, stage or radio plays, TV and film dramas.

➥ Write a couple of sentences about each of them and particularly about the pleasure, or otherwise, you had from them.

➥ See if there is a pattern of any sort here, and particularly notice if you are reading (or seeing or hearing) the sort of things you think you might want to write.

➥ Make a reading list for the next few weeks, emphasizing the sort of writing you feel you are most interested in producing yourself.

➥ At least once a month, bring the reading list from the second part of this exercise up to date and make comments on the new reading you have done.

The value of reading

This self-conscious reading should become a regular part of your own writing life. Keep coming back to this exercise and repeat the last part regularly; find people to talk about reading with. As you get involved with particular aspects of writing, like dialogue, or description, or pace, you will find yourself noticing more and more acutely how other writers handle these things. You will certainly learn from them, and will probably find that, apart from moments of jealousy and frustration, your own pleasure and interest in reading grows alongside your commitment to your own writing. This is an odd but extremely delightful spin off, a sort of free bonus that most people gain from thinking and working on writing – they become more creative readers.

You may hear some people say that reading is bad for writers – that it drowns their own unique voice and gets in the way of their originality. I do not agree. My own experience is quite the opposite: I think I forge my own style in the act of writing. Wide reading gives me a sense of companionship within a community of fellow writers; it gives me a sense of what is possible; it sets up challenges; and it gives me a unique insight into how readers read – and therefore how I (as a writer) can best communicate with them. At this stage on a writing journey reading will also give you a sense of what writing can do and what you might like to do with it. It is very like the child learning to speak whom I discussed in the opening chapter: no one thinks for a moment that a child will say more original and creative things if they never hear anyone talking to them.

Everyone needs to pour their sense of enthusiasm and their new energy for writing into some mould that can hold and shape it – this is why wide reading (even including the yoghurt pots) is so important. Of course no single writer can provide you with a model

to 'copy' but collectively they can teach you about the craft, giving you constant examples of what works (and what doesn't) and they can also give you a sense of where your own writing might slot in to this enormous range of books.

Stories

So it really is worth thinking and re-thinking the whole question of what writing you are going to work on next. Some people will find that the exercises in this book, and the notebooks they create, will satisfy them for a long time. Others need to have a clear framework, a sort of background to lay the exercises onto, or they find the work frustrating and pointless. You have to follow your own knowledge about the sort of person you are to create a balanced working practice that keeps you moving forward and also keeps you open and alive to the possibilities.

Because in another deeper sense the different forms do not mean much: in the end it is all *stories*.

Human beings seem to have some profoundly shared characteristics of mind as well as of body. Just as all human beings, unlike our simian relatives, have noses; so all human beings seem to have an innate desire to find patterns and order in the world around them. We seem to like mysteries, puzzles, and magic. It is not simply that we see patterns; it is that we impose them on anything that does not clearly have them already.

Exercise 16 Impose a pattern

☞ Opposite is a picture of a section of the night sky. All cultures have found pictures in the stars – even though realistically the Great Bear does not look remotely like a bear and Orion's belt could be almost anything.

➥ Remember that the stars change on a daily basis (like the moon and like the seasons). In the course of the night they also appear to move across the sky.

➥ Look at this particular area of stars very carefully for at least two whole minutes; just look at the stars and the dark spaces between them. (This will be much more difficult to do if you do, in fact, know anything about astronomy.)

➥ Take your pencil and (just as you did in those join-the-dot pictures when you were a child) join some stars together so that they form a picture.

➥ Write a story explaining why that picture is in the sky. It can be a *fiction* story; or it can be a tiny snippet of autobiography.

The point is that you have imposed a pattern, a story, on some thing that you, in your rational and modern mind, *know* to be random.

It isn't just that this sort of pattern-making is quite easy to do: it is astonishingly hard *not* to do it.

Language is linear

A story in its crude form is just a list of events linked together. The primary question 'what next' is answered by the implicit phrase 'and then. . .and then. . .'. The events are put into a satisfying order.

This list of events may explain the great mysteries – we call these lists 'myths', and they have evolved into poetry.Or they may amuse or explain something about other people (and ourselves) – we call these fiction.

Or they may impart practical information, moral values or education – we call these non-fiction. They are all stories.

The point is that this is what language does. It is linear: it says something and then it says the next thing. A picture does something different because you do not have to look at it in a linear way: you can look at tiny details, then the whole, then start in one place, then focus on another in any order you choose. Music does something different because you can have two notes or more at the same time.

With writing only one thing can happen at a time and it happens before the next thing.

It begins to feel as though language and storytelling (in all its forms) grew up together and meet each other. This is certainly a more plausible story than the idea that language developed in order to help people hunt – because if so they would have gone for a sign language rather than noisy, game-warning spoken languages.

First there was singing, then telling, then writing, then reading. And then we got 'literature' and it started being divided up into all the forms I talked about above – and lots more that I haven't mentioned – but fundamentally it is all stories in the simple sense that something happens and then something else happens.

So if you find a particular sort of writing that appeals to you, fine: pursue it. But if you do not immediately discover a form that matches your voice, do not worry about it. Just keep writing. As soon as you start writing down words and linking them into sentences you are asking the basic question 'what next?' and answering 'and then'. You are making patterns and telling stories.

First there was singing, then telling, then writing, then reading

Chapter 4 Metaphor

Earlier I promised you a special chapter on metaphor, and here it is. You will remember that I explained that metaphor is a rhetorical device, a kind of language trick that compares two different things by speaking of one in terms of the other. Unlike a simile or analogy, metaphor asserts that one thing *is* another thing, not just that one is *like* another: I give an example:

> 'The mind is but a barren soil; a soil which is soon exhausted and will produce no crop, or only one, unless it be continually fertilized and enriched with foreign matter.'
>
> **Joshua Reynolds**

Here Reynolds does not say, 'The mind is *like* a barren soil'. He says, 'It *is* a barren soil'. At one level we know perfectly well that the mind is not a 'barren soil': it isn't dry and crumbly and sprinkling it with chemical fertilizer or digging in some organic compost will have no beneficial effect. At the metaphorical level however it works really well: we know that he is saying our minds need external stimulus in order to produce good ideas. In fact we know this in a richer, more imaginative and fuller emotional way than if he had just said, 'Human minds need external stimulus in order to produce good ideas'. The 'barren soil' metaphor works particularly well in this context because we can see his point in practice: the 'foreign matter' of the metaphor does indeed 'fertilize and enrich our minds'.

The word *metaphor* comes from Greek and it is constructed out of two words, which originally meant 'to transfer beyond' to another (or a higher) place. (Metaphysics – the science beyond or higher than physics – demonstrates the same language structure.)

In a very real way *this is what creative writing does*. This is what it is for. This is how it works. It conveys meaning, by transferring a set

and meaning

of words and physical images to a larger or higher mental framework. It transfers things into the heart, the imagination and the emotional mind which otherwise would only lurk about in the physical or intellectual part of us.

It is perfectly possible to write a description of something that does not transfer feelings to anywhere and is not meant to: the manual for running your washing machine would be less well written if it raised your thoughts to a universal washing machine, or even to the death of your great-aunt. But in some fundamental way a washing machine manual is not what we mean when we talk about creative writing. I certainly do not want to imply that there can be no descriptions of washing machines, or other domestic detail, in good creative writing. We know this is not true. But the description of the washing machine in the manual is to help you use your washing machine; a description of a washing machine in a poem or prose fiction or personal memoir is there for something beyond itself. It is not the washing machine that is different. The *writing* itself is of a different register and has a different purpose.

The washing machine in the manual is *this* particular washing machine doing its primary job of washing your clothes. The washing machine in the story is not there to wash clothes, but to build the plot, tell the reader about the characters, provide an image of domestic agitation, or *something*. Indeed I would go further – the plot and the characters themselves exist to transfer you to something larger, something more general, something of personal relevance to both the writer and the reader.

This relevance may be emotional – literature is one of the places where we train and educate our emotions. But equally the relevance may be intellectual. It is perfectly possible to write a tidy little essay explaining what, for example, 'love' is and why this matters. However

Creative writing... transfers things into the heart, the imagination and the emotional mind

such an essay probably will not zing in our imaginations, move our emotions (even to the point of tears) or remain in our memories in the way that *Romeo and Juliet* or *Gone with the Wind*, or any decently written poem or romance, will. The understanding that these stories give us, even though they are about a single couple, in totally different circumstances from our own as we read them, informs the whole idea we have of what 'love' and its consequences are.

In this sense every work of literature, every act of creative writing, is itself a metaphor. This is perhaps clearest in poetry, but at one level or another all writers are using language to transfer meaning from one level to another. Understanding a bit about metaphor is therefore a crucial part of being able to develop your own writing.

The funny thing is that as we write we make metaphors whether we mean to or not and whether we understand what we are doing or not. Because this is what language does. As I explained in the chapter on language, the particular word we use for a particular object is arbitrary but powerful. In a sense you could say that just naming something creates a metaphor – it transfers this particular example or instance of 'chair', 'table' or 'freedom' to a wider general meaning. It unites this particular thing – some-bits-of-wood-attached-at-odd-angles-which-enable-comfortable-sitting – to a larger general experience of sitting. Moreover the word transfers the meaning across time and space. If I want you to think about a chair I do not have to dismantle one and send it through the post – I can just name it.

Association

But at this basic level the transfer is not very interesting. It gets interesting when I use language not just to conjure up a duplicate idea in your mind, but when I use it to conjure up bigger more emotionally significant material. This happens through *association*.

In Chapter 2 we saw how words summon up visual and other images of the thing that they represent. We also looked at how they come with an invisible aura around them; we looked at how they have a shape and register and sound and rhythm.

But even more importantly than these, they also have *associations*. By this I mean that words make people think about, or feel things other than simply the surface meaning of the word, or a physical idea of it. The word 'love' for example may make you think about your partner or your child or ice cream or God. The word 'love' does not *mean* 'ice cream', but it is – in some people's minds – profoundly associated with 'ice cream'. If you pause to examine almost any word, it will make you think about lots of other things as well, some of them quite deeply buried and many of them with no actual or obvious physical connection to the word itself. It is not just abstract nouns that do this – very concrete ones do too. This is worth experimenting with.

Exercise 17 Find associations

☞ Find six blank sheets of paper. You can use your notebook for this, but you do need an empty page for each word. (Other words on the page will set up other associations.)

☞ Make a list of any six nouns. Try and find nouns from various different contexts. e.g.: SANDWICH, KNITTING, WAR, SERMON, DIAMOND, KETTLE. At this stage try and avoid high falutin' abstracts like 'democracy' or 'individualism'.

☞ In the middle of each page, in capital letters, write one of these nouns.

☞ For five minutes, without stopping, scribble down all the things that the word makes you think of – everything you associate with that word. With each association attach it back to the core word by circling it and drawing a line to the starting word. (This is so that you do not wander too far down the route of thinking of the associations with your associations. That's a different exercise. For now you want to do something that brings you back to the noun you are working with.)

☞ You should end up with a surprising number of little ideas floating round the central word. Those are the *associations* of that word for you.

☞ Go immediately to the next word on your list. Do exactly the same thing.

☞ When you have finished these six words, try it again with abstract nouns.

☞ Now look at each sheet and see what you have got. Think about the fact that you can make all these associations conscious and external (by writing them down) in just five minutes. This should give you some awareness of the complexity, range and depth that every noun carries with it, at least subliminally, every time you hear or read it.

☞ If possible, it is instructive to do this exercise with a colleague. Use the same words, and afterwards share your pages. Try and explain some of your odder associations to each other. See which ones you have in common.

Analyzing your answers

When you look at your paper you will probably see that there are various types of association. The more you do this sort of exercise the more types you will find you come up with. Some likely types are:

Descriptions: associations that expand or specify the imaginary 'kettle' you have in mind. (These are words like 'electric' or ' enamel'.)

Verbal associations: the word sounds like or reminds you of some other word (puns, rhymes, or jokes for instance).

Memories: fragments of stories about previous encounters with the word. (For example, 'kettle' = 'Granny's house'.)

Ideas: abstractions or intellectual content that the word brought up.

Inexplicable stuff: even immediately after completing the exercise you cannot work out what the association was.

Now strike out all the associations that are purely descriptive; the ones referring to a particular kettle that you happened to think of at the time. These descriptive phrases may well be useful elsewhere, but for the moment they are not the substance of metaphor.

Association and the writer

There is a good chance that some associations will be so personal that they are obscure and will not easily work the transfer for anyone except you. I could have written:

'The mind is but a drunken tortoise, propelled forever on the blue merry-go-round; a tortoise softened by immersion in bleach.'

I might even, with a long explanation, be able to demonstrate the sources of my personal association of minds, tortoises, merry-go-rounds and bleach. But it is still not a very useful metaphor, unlike Reynold's, because the associations are too personal, too eccentric and do not overlap *enough* with the reader's associations for them to convey much meaning.

Equally some of the associations are likely to be almost universal, trite and not very interesting. I could also have written:

> 'The mind is but a machine; a machine that needs regular oiling in order to work smoothly.'

This clearly is a 'sensible' and entirely straightforward association. But it is not a strong metaphor because a good number of readers will already have thought about the ways in which the mind is and is not like a machine. This association is unlikely to give any new insight or mental thrill because it overlaps *too much* with the reader's own associations, and so will not move them to any new perception.

In between these two is the place where the real writing happens. The place where, by means of a basically simple language *trick*, the reader is transferred from one set of meanings to another, which is beyond the apparent range of the sentence – from the particular to the general, from the known to the unknown.

Not all writers do this very consciously. For some people it happens very early in a writing process. They find a story, a character or an image that they attach to themselves very strongly and they write about it and only realize afterwards (if at all) what it was actually *about*. Other writers do it very consciously indeed – they go looking for the metaphor to match their abstract subject matter in a quite deliberate way. Most of us I suspect muddle along with various moments of illumination, a good deal of instinct and some buried but burning things we want to write about.

...by means of a simple language trick, the reader is transferred from one set of meanings to another

'Buried' metaphors

Clearly the ability to make metaphors and therefore to understand them is rather a sophisticated mental process, and whichever group of *Homo sapiens* first deployed this odd device was creative at a very profound level. Nonetheless once the idea caught on it became absolutely essential to the full working of language. This is so much the case that many of the words we use, even in the washing machine manual are in fact, on inspection, 'buried' metaphors.

The warm sun *caressed* her body.
The old lady was *tending* her fire.
His complaint was *trivial.*
There is a *biting* wind.
He strained his *Achilles tendon.*
She sobbed *hysterically.*
My *heart* was *touched.*
We need to *iron* out these problems.

If you cannot see why I am calling any of these phrases 'metaphors' look the words in italics up in an etymological dictionary – one that gives you the history and derivation of the words. (For instance the wind has no teeth, so to describe it as 'biting' is a tiny metaphor.)

Exercise 18 Find and use metaphors

➪ Take the front page of any tabloid newspaper and read it with care, highlighting any metaphorical language you can find.

➪ Take any piece of your own writing and do the same thing.

➪ The purpose behind this is to demonstrate that 'metaphor' is not some high literary art, but is embedded in the way we all speak and write; it is absolutely central to any vivid, powerful and meaningful writing. However it is also a short cut to sloppy cliché-ridden writing. It is therefore something that you need to become aware of so that you, as the writer, can take control.

☞ Take a long and careful look out of the nearest window – write a descriptive passage of the scene, including the weather. (Writing about the weather nearly always involves metaphors.) Aim for about 500–1,000 words.

☞ Highlight all the words that you have used metaphorically; include single words and phrases. If you aren't sure, look up the word in the dictionary.

☞ Write a description of the same scene using no metaphors.

☞ Compare the two and see which you prefer. There is no right or wrong in such matters, but very few writers would choose to avoid *all* metaphorical language *all* of the time.

Metaphor and the reader

Although metaphor is omnipresent in language, many people find themselves self-conscious when they try to invent metaphors and insert them into their writing. One danger with this sort of self-consciousness is the desire to point out to the reader, directly or indirectly, what you are doing. But making generalizations from your own metaphors is always a mistake. If you have got the metaphor right the reader will be able, at some level, to sense it. If you have not got it right, the less they notice it the better.

The poet William Carlos Williams once described his approach to poetry with the phrase, 'no ideas but in things'. He meant that you did not need to explain yourself or create abstractions and generalizations and fancy ideas. If you show the reader the physical *things* that you have truly observed rather than fancy ideas you have hammered onto those things, then they will do the 'transferring' for you. A powerful piece of writing is always teamwork: respect your readers, and you will find there is nothing to be self-conscious about.

To put this important point a slightly different way: Shakespeare does not have to begin *Romeo and Juliet* by saying 'this is a play about teenage love and its problems. The two central characters are metaphors for young people everywhere, and all the other characters are metaphors for the stupid things we say and do to teenage lovers'. He tells us a quite specific story about two specific teenagers who are surrounded by assorted friends and family who are all – because of their personalities or social roles – involved in a tragedy.

The writer's job is with the *things*; the reader's job is with the meaning. The writer needs to stay as close as possible to the actual concrete reality of the senses and the emotions, and leave the lofty generalizations well alone.

Exercise 19 Create extended metaphors

☞ In your notebook write down three *ideas* that interest you. They might be purely intellectual ideas, for example: 'Cantor proves that infinity comes in different sizes'. But they are more likely to be social or emotional ideas like, 'The sort of childhood we have affects the sort of adults we become'; 'The freedom of the press is necessary for democracy'; 'Rainy days depress me'; 'Eating other people is wrong.'

➭ Create an extended metaphor for some of the words in each of your ideas: *An extended metaphor is one like that of Reynolds at the beginning of this section – he starts by saying 'The mind is a barren soil', and then extends the metaphor by assuming his readers have some idea of what barren soil might actually involve ('one crop or none') and how fertilizer might improve the situation.* Therefore, an extended metaphor for the word 'infinity' might be:

> 'Struggle with the mathematics though I may, infinity remains for me writing without punctuation – intriguing, exciting, challenging but, sadly, very hard work to read and ultimately impossible to make sense of. I am convinced there is beauty and wisdom in it, but I cannot decode it. Angels may sing continuously without pause for breath, and so without need of punctuation; but I cannot find the grammar of its meaning.'

Of course this is simply *my* metaphor, and an example of how you might think about it, not how you might write it. But what you are aiming for is an 'explanation' which opens up ideas rather than answering all the questions.

➭ You might find it interesting, even if you do not think of yourself as someone who writes poetry, to try and arrange your metaphor into lines, rhythms or patterns, or make a poem. However, in doing so, check that you stick to the physical reality of the thing you have chosen. Don't generalize or moralize.

☞ Think of a story that would illustrate the abstract idea you are interested in. Imagine characters who would be metaphors for different sides of the argument, or a situation that could drive your message home. Make notes about how you could tell such a story and which characters and situations you might require.

☞ Try this with several different ideas. Think about which ones work best as verbal descriptive metaphors, and which ones would profit from fully developed plots, with characters and episodes.

☞ REMEMBER that this is an *exercise*. Great writing does not really happen like this. Some of the best literature is written precisely because the writers did not know what they thought and so wrote in order to find out. Modern readers are not usually very engaged with 'fables' – stories that simply illustrate a moral. Your own gut instinct will be more valuable in finding the associations that will work for your writing than this sort of exercise ever can be. The point is to understand what is going on, so that you can use it instead of being sucked into a whirlpool of confusion.

The point that I am making here is simple. Metaphor – the ability of language to 'transfer meaning beyond' itself – is what makes creative writing (as opposed to all the other kinds) work. It works by triggering associations and links in the reader's mind. It works at every level, from word, through phrase, sentence, character and plot to the whole piece of writing seen as a seamless unity. You need to think about it, try to understand it and use it to your own ends in your writing.

Chapter 5 Now tell

You may be thinking that it is all very well to claim, as I now have, that everything we write or say is already a unique and valuable story, and is rich in meaning and metaphor. This is entirely true, at one level, but presumably you did not buy this book just to be reassured that your every utterance and scribble was already great writing. I presume that at least one of the reasons why you have worked your way this far into the book and, indeed, that one of the reasons why you want to write, is precisely because you want to go beyond what you are already able to do. You want to explore that shadowy territory where writing moves into a higher gear and becomes something more than chat, or inchoate private burblings. You want your writing to become not just a way of letting off steam or venting your personal frustrations, but a subtle and sharp instrument of complex communication. You want, in short, to learn the craft skills of writing; in the same way as our potter from earlier in the book does indeed need clay, but also needs to know how to handle and shape the clay on the wheel, how to apply the glazes and heat the kiln.

Can writing be taught?

You have to understand that there is no 'right' or 'wrong' way of writing. There is no magic spell that will make your writing wonderful. The skills are nebulous and hard earned. There are some things that really cannot be taught – although they can be learned.

The only way to acquire these skills is to write and read, and read and write. You need to experiment and keep experimenting. Luckily writing is a reasonably safe pursuit: unlike solo flying the consequences of getting it wrong are extremely mild. You could probably glean all the teaching and information that you need through systematic and thoughtful reading. Indeed, until

your stories

comparatively recently, this was almost the only way of learning how to write.

Nonetheless, more recently there has been a great deal of thought about particular skills and techniques, and about how to learn and develop them. There is now a body of experience and agreement about some aspects of writing and how to achieve excellence. In this chapter we are going to look in some detail at some of these aspects. In order to talk about them sensibly and usefully it is necessary to isolate them. This has some problems, because, to take a simple example, 'how to present character' depends in the end on the context, on the whole piece of writing in which the character is being presented. Perhaps there are no characters in what you want to write; perhaps you are a person who has no difficulty with this aspect of creative writing anyway. Even if you do want to think about this and other techniques, they may come up in a completely different order from the one I am going to use. The whole thing is troublesome and can be rather frustrating.

What I recommend is that you read through the whole of this chapter so that you know what is in it. You will get a general feel for the sort of approach I am suggesting and you may get some flashes of inspiration. Something I have written in it may trigger something in your own imagination. But after that you should feel free to use it as a resource. If you have a specific problem, question, or something you know you need to work more on, come back to that section and work your way through the exercises there. If you are, at some time in the future, feeling stuck or depressed about your writing, take a section almost at random and try those exercises along with the ones in the previous chapters.

Do not treat this chapter as though it were an instruction manual. Do not feel that you must slog laboriously through the whole thing,

The only way to acquire [creative writing] skills is to write and read, read and write page by page. In the long run it is probably a good idea to get hold of further books, especially if you have settled down to working within a particular form, and compare or contrast that author's ideas with mine. I see this chapter, particularly, as more like a recipe book than a textbook. You don't have to sit down and cook your way through every page of a recipe book. You can go to the general section (supper, puddings, snacks, whatever) and skim through the various offerings there until you find something that appeals to you, or matches the ingredients you want to use. Then you read that one recipe in detail and follow the instructions.

'Page turnability'

Obviously there are more things I might write about, more techniques and approaches, more skills and tricks, more challenges and consolations, than there would be room for in any volume. I cannot hope to cover everything. Recently a group of creative writing MA students I have taught came up with a list of qualities that they felt were essential for what you might call 'page turnability' – those things that make a reader want to read on. They came up with a list of five essential qualities:

❖ Plausible, authentic characters that readers can identify with.
❖ Trustworthy authorial voice and point of view.
❖ Conflict and suspense.
❖ Variety.
❖ Persuasive, evocative descriptions.

Of course page turnability is not the only criterion of great writing, but this list seems to me to provide me with a useful selection of skills, so I am going to use it. I will take each item in turn and look at ways of developing each of these aspects of your work.

It is worth noticing that this group was actually discussing novels, so it may be that not everything on this list will be necessary to you. Nonetheless, most of these characteristics will apply in one way or another to all kinds of writing.

CHARACTERS

As we saw above, the students concluded that characters were *essential* to a novel. Many people would go further than this and claim that a novel's central characters have to be more than simply present – they also should show at least *some* of the following qualities: plausibility; being interesting or surprising; likeable; and above all capable of being identified with.

The novel is indeed the place where the 'fully rounded character' performs best. Most novels are based around the idea that people are complex but coherent, and that this complexity is what determines what happens to them. From the traditional 'fatal flaw' through to the slushiest romance, the novel depends on the idea that the sort of character someone is affects what happens to him or her. Characters drive the story. Whether or not we believe this in real life is irrelevant.

But it is not just the novel that needs characters: drama, short stories, even poems require characters. In a poem, the character is very often the 'voice of the poet' – but that is a 'fiction' too, something that the poet makes up, however truthfully, out of selected fragments of a complex identity. One might argue that the challenges around character in these other forms are greater than they are for the novelist – because their writers have to supply the same depth with far less obvious tools. Dramatists have to illuminate the inner life of the characters entirely through what they say and do;

short stories have to compress information and usually leave out explanatory background material, and the poet has to walk a tight-rope between truth and form.

Characters in fiction are not exactly the same as people in real life. There are a number of reasons for this and here are a few of them:

- ❖ Other people are essentially unknowable to us. However intimately we are connected, in the end there is a deep mystery about other people. We cannot know everything and we know we do not know everything. What writing about other people can do is transcend that mystery: writing presents us with people we do know about *fully*. We know their inmost thoughts, their exact feelings and even aspects of their subconscious of which they are not aware. This, I think, is the reason why fictional characters can stick in one's mind more vividly and more permanently than real people. This sense of penetrating the mystery and truly knowing someone is one of the great pleasures of reading and is certainly one of the expectations that, consciously or unconsciously, readers bring with them when they approach new writing.

- ❖ Most people in daily life do not spend their time thinking about, and acting through, emotional relationships. They spend the bulk of their days sleeping, eating, attending to their personal maintenance (washing, dressing and so on), working and doing absolutely nothing at all worth mentioning. Characters in books, however, do little of any of these 'real life' activities; they live in a world of relationship and emotion – so that even 'lazing about' takes on meaning and significance.

❖ Real life is littered with coincidence, accident and diversions from 'the plot'. Large parts of each day and each year and even whole decades have nothing much to do with the story of an individual life – and death may come at a point which is arbitrary and resolves nothing. A life has a story but it may not have a plot – in the sense of a clear trajectory that ends with some sort of satisfying closure. Characters, however, live through plots: the fewer coincidences, the fewer accidents, the fewer irrelevant events or insignificant characters they encounter the better. Their story always ends at a significant point and the ending (whatever it is) resolves something that has been there all along.

The problem is that at the same time that all these things are perfectly true, readers also want to be able to believe that the characters in books *are* real – that they are plausible, authentic and capable of being identified with. So writers have a very difficult conjuring trick to pull off.

Luckily writers also have a number of factors that work to their advantage:

The reader is on your side

The first is that, provided the other elements of the book are strong enough, the reader is on the writer's side. They want to enjoy the book they are reading – and so they will accept a reasonable amount of coincidence, accident and irrelevance. They will even accept a certain amount of improbability if they are enjoying the book. (We know this, as readers, because if some writer fails to engage us we become immensely picky and particular about minor details.)

You know yourself

The second is that there is someone that we know more about than we do about anyone else in the world – our self. We know our own most secret dreams and aspirations and we also know with great precision what our own headache *actually feels like*. We know ourselves in a similar way to the way we know fictional characters. So if we are honest about ourselves we can in fact perform the trick that the writing requires. Of course this does mean there is no good writing without rigorous self-examination and a good deal of courageous *honesty*. This does not mean that all the characters we ever write about are just the same – because one of the things we know about ourselves is that we are not completely coherent and consistent. We can ask different aspects of our self for the resources to construct our characters out of. Nor, interestingly, does it mean that we can only write about what we have actually experienced – we can write about space travel or child murder provided we link it somehow to our own knowledge of our own self.

I was discussing this with my daughter who is an actor. 'Yes,' she said, 'that is what Method Acting is – the engagement that allows you to find a link between your real self and the character you are going to act. It can take a lot of research and self-examination but the link is almost always there if you put in the work.' I find this helpful.

Characters develop

The third, and perhaps the most important, factor is that characters have a way of revealing themselves as you write them. For many writers this leads to a feeling that the characters are somehow writing themselves – that they have taken control of the writing or, at least, are somehow sharing the job with the writer.

'And I thank my characters for coming,' Alice Walker wrote in the acknowledgements section of *The Color Purple*. Not all writers feel this way. I personally would never let my characters get so far out of control that I could not take responsibility for them – and bend them to the needs of my story as a whole. Yet I still know that once a story is well established the characters (and the images and the language itself) start to teach me things about themselves that I, when thinking about them, would not have come up with and did not plan on.

It does not matter how many notes you take, or how much thought you give to the characters before you start writing, you will always find that they surprise you if you are writing honestly. This does mean that once you get going your characters will become more and more real to you – and you will find it easier and easier to show them to the reader.

So far this is really just background. Now I am going to look at some technical props and supports – as it were the equipment for the conjuring trick. I will be giving some quite specific 'instructions'. If you feel doubtful about whether anything I am saying is right for you in any particular writing circumstance, stop thinking of yourself as a writer for a moment and try to think of yourself as a reader. 'If I were reading about this character would I like it this way? Trust it this way?' This is an excellent test. It does mean though that you have to trust yourself as a reader – an additional reason for developing the kind of reading practice I was talking about earlier.

Introducing a new character

I am going to begin at the beginning and start with how you might introduce a new character. Here, as indeed elsewhere, the rule is:

Show, don't tell

We can ask different aspects of ourself for the resources to construct our characters

How do you get to know a real person? The answers are 'gradually' and 'through what they say and do'. When you meet a new person in 'real life' they do not hand you a list of their main characteristics, nor do they stand completely still for five minutes while you inspect and measure them and note exactly how tall they are, what colour their eyes are and what their parents' jobs were. They give you a first impression, and then – if you are interested – you start to pick up other points about their appearance, and through observation and often through conversation you gradually learn more about them.

Yet how often when we start writing new characters do we create a sort of freeze-frame moment in which we describe at totally unnecessary length their appearance, past history and moral values? You may well feel that *you* need to know quite a lot of things about your character before you start writing – their height or hair colour may be important so that you can choreograph your action (two tall people can see each other across a crowded room for example). It may be crucial to the story you are telling that the character's mother was a doctor. But those sorts of lists belong in your notebook, not on your written page. Anything that the reader needs to know should be fed to them through actions and conversations.

Exercise 20 Develop a character

➯ Think about a character you would like to write about. (If you kept those photographs I suggested you put in your scrapbook, you can use one of them for inspiration here.)

➯ Make a list in your notebook of five things about this character that you think are interesting or important. If you can think of two which are visible physical characteristics (height, clothes, complexion etc.); two which are personality traits (impatience, intelligence, generosity and so on); and one which is something about his or her past or social role (orphan, managing director, very rich, etc.) that will be helpful.

☞ Write a few scenes (or a single scene if you can manage it) in which all five items on your list are shown through the actions or conversations of the characters. *Show* the reader these characteristics, rather than *telling* the reader what the characteristics are. (Remember that the reactions of other characters can be 'showing'. Compare these two sentences: 'Amanda always dressed smartly' and 'As soon as she saw Amanda, Elspeth felt dowdy'. In the second, we see Amanda's 'smartness' through the reaction of another character. Apart from this being more like 'real life' it has the advantage that in a single sentence you have told the reader something about Elspeth as well as about Amanda – two for the price of one, so to speak.)

☞ If, in the course of writing the exercise, you suddenly 'learn' something new about your character add it to the list. When you have completed the five items you started with, write another scene showing this new fact or detail through action or conversation.

☞ Keep adding to the list and writing more scenes until nothing new is coming up.

Obviously there are times when the writer is just going to have to pop up and give away some information. This may be for reasons of economy – for instance to move the story from one scene to another without too much digression it may be better simply to *tell* the reader that, 'The next day he went to Edinburgh by train' rather than *show* a whole six-hour journey through the actions and thoughts of the character. Perhaps none of the characters you have on hand know the fact that needs to be given to the reader. But as a general rule it is always better, not just in an introduction but throughout a piece of writing, to show a thing happening rather than to tell the reader it has happened.

- ❖ 'She was in agony' is *telling* the reader something.
- ❖ 'She was writhing on the floor moaning' is *showing* them something.
- ❖ And so, interestingly, is '"I'm in agony," she whimpered'.

Here the 'whimpered' is giving the reader extra information about the sort of agony she is in. She might, for example, have *screamed*, *gasped* or *sobbed* – or if you wanted to show that she was very brave she could even have *announced*.

Although it is less obvious, speaking is an action by the character not an observation by the writer.

Writing in the first person

If you are writing in the first person you have an additional complication. People *simply do not* walk along thinking to themselves: 'My name is Elizabeth Brown. I have fair hair, and am 5 feet, 4 inches tall. I am thirty-four years old and work as a salesgirl in a department store. My father, James Brown, would have been disappointed, as I was his pride and joy, but he died when I was fifteen and my family was very short of money.' Writing in the first person always seems as though it should be easier – but like any other decision it has its own difficulties.

'First person' means that the storyteller uses 'I'. Usually the 'I' narrator is inside the story. 'Third person' means using 'he', 'she' and 'they'; this sort of a narrator tends to be outside the story, rather than a character in it. There is also 'second person' which means that the storyteller uses 'you'. This is more unusual, at least for longer pieces. The usual term for the storyteller is 'the narrator'. These are just handy agreed ways of talking about how a story is told. I shall look a bit more at these in the section on 'point of view'.

The main point about this 'showing not telling' rule is that it allows a character to feel like a real person to the reader. It has an additional important advantage though – it keeps the story moving forward more dynamically. (Imagine going to a film where every time a new character came on the film stopped and a voice-over told you a few important facts about that character.)

Getting to know your characters

If your central characters are going to feel truly knowable and alive to the reader then you yourself will have to know a lot about them. You will probably know more than you ever need to tell. I have already suggested that you learn more about them by writing about them. Nevertheless this process needs to be a little self-conscious. You have to acquire the knack of listening to your own writing and realizing when the characters are telling you something useful and important and when you and they are just slightly bored and 'messing around'. There is one way of doing this which makes a useful exercise, especially if the writing feels stuck and you sense that the energy is draining away from your work. It is called 'interrogating your character' and many writers (including me) find this great fun, as well as very useful. The idea is to get a more detailed and active sense of your character, by imagining that you are cross-questioning them.

Exercise 21 Interrogate your character

☞ Think about one of the central characters in your writing; think about everything you have written about them so far, and about where the story is heading (even if you are not entirely sure of the exact end yet).

☞ In your notebook make a few rough headings about the things you know about yourself that no one else knows or the things that you enjoy discovering about your close friends.

☞ Draw up a list of ten questions about these sorts of things. Here is a sample list that I use sometimes, but remember that what is relevant for my characters may not be at all applicable to yours. This list would not work for a Martian or a Neolithic cave dweller and you would have to think of different questions.

1) What was her/his favourite teddy-bear (or similar) called?
2) If money were no object where would s/he most like to go on holiday?
3) What single word/phrase would s/he be most likely to use if s/he banged an elbow (hard)?
4) What was her/his favourite subject in her/his last year of primary school?
5) Who does s/he hate/dislike most in the world?
6) What kind of shoes does s/he own?)

7) When did s/he last see her/his mother? Was it enjoyable?

8) Does s/he know the maiden names of her/his grandmothers?

9) What is her/his favourite food? Who cuts/styles her/his hair? Does s/he enjoy this?

10) What animal would you (the author) compare her/him to? What animal would s/he compare her/himself to?

☞ Think hard about these questions (or about your own list). Brood on them. Write the answers down. If you take your time you may find that just thinking about the question actually throws up the most compelling details about a character.

☞ Jot down any other interesting ideas you have, even if they don't directly answer the specific questions.

☞ Read what you have already written about this character. Does this new information make anything feel less satisfactory than before?

☞ In your notebook write briefly about how you felt about doing this exercise. What have you learned about your character? How might that affect the way you are writing?

Characters are essential and as you develop your writing you will have to wrestle with them. The more you are alert to how people (including yourself) actually *are*: how they walk and sit and smile and speak; how they dream and work and hope. . .every little detail you notice will strengthen your hand when you come to mould them into the fabric of your writing.

This is where the notebook and the journal can be invaluable. On a daily basis you should be jotting down things that you see and hear and think about how and what human beings do.

Exercise 22 Record life's material

☛ This is not, like the other exercises so far, a one-off. It is ongoing and needs constant development and updating, but here is a list of the sorts of things that – when opportunity presents itself – are well worth writing about.

☛ When you meet a new person write about your own reactions to them. Try and analyse why you had those reactions.

☛ When you meet an old friend or acquaintance try and notice something new about them – either something that has changed or something that you had never thought of before. Very tiny things count here – a new haircut or a new jersey will do; but as you get into practice you will notice more and more. Try to distinguish between things that are new to the person and things that are new to you. (X is unlikely to have suddenly developed wrinkles today. Think about when this happened and why you haven't noticed them before.) This exercise is most useful with people that you see regularly.

☛ Watch someone doing a job of work: the bus driver, the supermarket till checker, the road digger. Observe yourself doing jobs too – cooking, washing, eating. Write about it.

☛ If you keep a journal of your daily life, pick a single episode out of it and write it as though someone quite different were going through the same actions. A child, a drunk, a dog. Even just moving from the journal's first person to a third-person narrative, or from the present to the past tense will focus your attention on character.

☞ Write down a bit of conversation you have overheard. Then write a brief life story for the speaker.

☞ Set yourself challenges; do new things. Write about them. There are two reasons behind this exercise. One is that, if you look at the list the students made you will see that conflict and suspense were their second most essential quality, so you especially need to explore your own feelings and experiences of conflict and suspense. Doing something you have never done before (go up in a hot-air balloon; make a bet on a horse; read a new type of book; anything at all that is new and challenging) will inevitably provoke those feelings very effectively. The second reason is that the more alive you are to everything that goes on around you – in your mind and in the world – the more your writing will come alive to you, and the more your characters will come alive to your future readers.

Always remember, though, that the readers need these characters to feel 'plausible and authentic' so they can identify with them. If you are alive to yourself you will be quite well aware that you are neither an angel of light nor a pit of pestilent evil. You are, just within each single day, a complex mixture of aspiration, achievement and laziness; of dark and light. The worst villains in the world are kind to their pet goldfish, or pause in their infamy long enough to be genuinely moved by a small child or a spring morning. The most

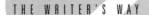
noble and virtuous of us still have moments of smugness or ill humour. Because at some level we all know this to be *true*, readers will not find one-dimensional characters authentic and they almost certainly won't be capable of identifying with them. And as a result, characters' conversation is very important from this respect too.

Characters' conversation

The proper creative writing word for conversation is 'dialogue'. Originally this word meant two people talking together, but it has come to mean written-down conversation in writing or dramatic speech – plays, films and so on – even if there are more than two people involved. I am going to call it conversation here, but dialogue as a word does have one real purpose. It makes clear that conversation written down in a novel, story, play, film, memoir or poem is not the same as ordinary social conversation.

You may be surprised that conversation does not have its own category in the students' list that I mentioned earlier. This is partly because conversation is not *essential* to a novel. I can think of novels that have no conversation or direct speech in them whatsoever, although this is quite rare. Readers *like* conversations – it is one of the features that distinguish creative writing from more prosaic kinds of reading. At the very basic level it breaks up the page (remember what I was saying about shape in language, in Chapter 3, p. 58) so that it looks easier and more inviting. It also helps the writer meet two of the other criteria which the students did think were essential – variety and engaging use of language.

...conversation is not essential to a novel

But I also suspect that the reason 'conversation' is not on their list is because it is so fundamental a part of developing and showing the characters. One of the things that people do – it is an action – is speak to each other. It is an important part of how we relate to other people and how we learn more about who they are and what makes them tick. It is a crucial tool in *showing* the characters in action, rather than *telling* the reader about them. This is why I am putting some ideas about it in here.

Writing conversations strikes terror into the hearts of a great many writers. Some of this is technical – the rules for writing down conversation, and particularly for punctuating it, feel like minefields: at any moment we will make some ghastly error and the teacher's red pen in our heads will pounce down exposing our ignorance and incompetence.

But the real reason why it feels difficult is much simpler than this – it is difficult.

Learning from emails

In 'real life', conversations, or most of all conversations, are 'babble'. When people talk to each other they use a very small vocabulary, which they back up with stock phrases, complex signs, gestures, facial clues, conventional padding and a general agreement to try and understand. They also use an entirely different sort of grammar: for example, not completing sentences and replacing punctuation marks with changes of tone or volume. The emerging etiquette in emails shows how separate the two ways of communicating (spoken and written language) actually are. Emails endeavour to reproduce *speech* – they are quick, immediate and intimate. But typed out they are also very hard to read correctly. 'Flaming', the phenomenon where fights escalate very, very quickly in chat rooms and group discussions has made people realise how much we modulate our actual spoken words with other information. 'You idiot' can be *spoken* affectionately, humorously, slightly irritably and downright insultingly; but nothing of that nuanced inflection comes over when the word is *read*, rather than heard. At first people got around that problem with little typographical games – like the smiling face :-) to show that the intention was humorous. Now indeed, if I try and type in that code my computer automatically reproduces it as ☺. This is called an 'emoticon' – a rather splendid new word combining 'emotion' and 'icon'. But as a writer, beware of these. As writers we want to claim that written language can carry all the meaning of spoken language and carry it further and for longer. The whole piece of writing needs to be an emoticon – we are not really allowed to add them in. In fact I personally would be rather irritated if a series of funny signs in the margin of a book I was reading instructed me about what the writer wanted me to feel. I would feel that the writer was simply not up to the job.

Writing conversation

When we write conversations we are trying to show in one sort of language something that really happens in another sort of language. That is the first difficulty. There are more: in real conversations, a good deal of what is said is about nothing of any significance whatsoever. Long rambling mealtime conversations include diversions, digressions and abrupt total changes of direction. This will not do for writing. Written conversations have to *feel* like spoken conversations, but at the same time they have to:

- ❖ Reveal character
- ❖ Move the story forward
- ❖ Stick to the point
- ❖ Make sense to a third party (the reader)
- ❖ Be stimulating and interesting and meaningful throughout
- ❖ Not go on indefinitely.

Exercise 23 Write down a conversation

☞ Tape-record a conversation. (Morally you ought to ask people's permission before you do this.) The best conversations for this purpose are those of small groups, with perhaps four to six people, who know each other fairly well. Meals are particularly useful. You probably want to record about an hour's worth of ordinary 'real' conversation.

☞ On a separate occasion, listen to the whole tape. Unless you already have the skills and equipment, transcribing everything on such a tape is a time-consuming activity. There is no need to do it. Practise careful listening instead, which will be a far more valuable exercise.

☞ Think about whether what I have written above is true of this conversation.

☞ Make notes on the different ways each of the individual people speak.

☞ Write down what the conversation was about. There will probably be more than one topic. Try to summarise the hour.

☞ Try and write a version of the conversation in about 1,000 words. You can leave out all the 'he saids' and 'she murmureds'. Just give each voice a letter or number and put it at the beginning of each person's words, like a play script.

☞ Write some notes on the differences between the tape and your written version.

Among other things you will probably find that you have got:

❖ Some distinct and vivid expressions. They may be new ways of expressing something, or a turn of phrase that is somehow typical of the speaker. These are the things you want to keep; make sure you write them down in your notebook as accurately as possible.

❖ A good deal of repetition, especially of stock phrases and expressions (clichés); a lot of 'filler' words (things like *um*, *I mean*, and *but look* – and so on). These are usually things you want to lose, although it is worth noticing how much they do come up.

❖ Extremely tangled and knotted strands of ideas and subject matter. These you need to comb out and organize.

❖ Inexplicable interruptions – often about the physical reality of what is going on. People dropping things, passing plates and other activities which do not seem to break up the conversation on the tape but will break it up on the page. You need to think about these strategically – do they add enough to the characters or the realism to be worth losing the thread of the ideas?

❖ More than one person talking at a time. It is impossible to write this down accurately. Even if you write 'They were all talking at once', you still have to decide whose words to record *first*. Because of the linear nature of language, you can never show two things happening simultaneously. It is a limitation you just have to deal with as best you can.

A note on accents. It is very tempting to try and reproduce people's accents by spelling out their speech phonetically. This used to be a very normal practice – especially with rustic or working-class people. But unless you have a remarkably good ear (and a good understanding of phonetics) – be careful. There are people who are very good indeed at this (Irving Welsh in Trainspotting *for example) and if you are not as precise as such experts, people will notice instantly. Moreover written English is not phonetic in its spelling – so you either have to represent* everyone's *accents, or you will find you have, willy-nilly, said something political about who speaks properly in 'standard English'. My own view is that it is better to suggest regional and class-based speakers through the vocabulary and rhythm of their written speech than by the wild dropping of 'h's and similar tricks, unless you have a very clear purpose in mind.*

The main purpose of this exercise is to teach yourself why writing conversations is so hard. Once you are fully aware of the problem, forget it. Or at least do not be afraid of it. You will have read lots and lots of books in which conversations took place – and on the whole you will not have noticed the problem. The readers, like writers, are subconsciously attuned to written conversation not being exactly like spoken conversation. They will go along with this particular literary fiction quite happily. The danger comes when writers lose control and are so keen to put the ideas over that they let their own voice slip into the characters' voices, or give the characters vast and unwieldy, beautifully grammatical but completely unnatural 'speeches' to make. (One version of this is giving the reader information through conversations, which the characters would never need to give to each other – for example, 'Elizabeth who is my forty-six-year-old mother-in-law and your youngest sister...'.) Readers will only go so far.

A good rule of thumb (although of course there will be exceptions) is that in normal 'naturalistic' conversation, no one should speak for more than about four lines of typing without other characters coming in.

The best way I know to develop your writing skills in this important but tricky area is to work on a radio play, or scenes for a radio play. In radio you have *nothing* except conversation (plus possibly some background sounds to help with the mood). Here conversation has to do very nearly unaided all the things that elsewhere it can find help with: reveal the characters, create the plot, provide the ideas, make sense to the listeners *and* be stimulating and interesting and meaningful throughout.

Exercise 24 Write a radio play

➡ Think of a dramatic story. The important thing here is to come up with a situation which has a good deal of movement and activity attached to it: a car breakdown; a barbeque; a highjacking for example.

➡ Imagine the individual characters you need to be involved in this event. Try to think of a way of telling this story, which will not involve more than three or four characters.

➡ Write it as though it were a radio play. This means you cannot describe the place – except through background noise (a beach has very clear sounds, for example). You cannot describe the characters except through their voices (male, female, general indication of age and hints about their background). You cannot report their actions except through sounds, of which the main one will be what they say to each other.

☞ Find a group of people who are willing to read it through aloud with you.

☞ Discuss it with them. Are they comfortable saying their appointed parts? Are the words in fact *sayable*? Very long sentences and those with highly unnatural rhythms can be very difficult to say. If someone sitting calmly and trying to co-operate with you is struggling with a sentence, it is very unlikely that anyone in a dramatic situation would actually be able to use it. Can the group work out what is supposed to be happening? Do they have a good sense of the character they are reading out? Have you managed to make their conversation interesting?

Conversation takes practice. It is however entirely possible to learn how to write it. So:

❖ Practice
❖ Listen to the things people say and the way that they say them; eavesdrop shamelessly
❖ *Write* conversations down and experiment with different ways of handling them
❖ Read plays and go to the theatre, watch drama on the TV and listen to radio plays
❖ Read your own written conversations back to yourself aloud
❖ Notice how writers write their conversations
❖ Think about rhythm and vocabulary and character; keep notes on your thoughts.

And, quite simply, you will get better and better at it.

TRUSTWORTHY AUTHORIAL VOICE

Now I am going to move on from characters to writers themselves. Not their personalities, hang-ups and problems for a moment, but the writer as he or she appears *in the writing*. You may have noticed that in their list, the students used the phrase 'authorial voice' rather than 'author'. They saw a 'trustworthy authorial voice' as being essential to successful writing.

The reader–writer contract

When someone picks up a book or magazine and starts to read any piece of creative writing, they are entering into an implicit contract with the writer. They have committed time and money to the project and are entitled to set some terms and conditions.

A few of these terms have quasi-legal status. For example:

- ❖ The work has actually been written by the person whose name is on the cover – the writer has not stolen it from someone else (plagiarism; or breach of copyright).
- ❖ If the book claims to be a 'true story' it must be true (ish).
- ❖ If it claims to be a fiction it must not be about recognizable and identifiable real people.
- ❖ If, whether it claims to be fiction or non-fiction, it refers to real people it must not tell gratuitous lies about them (libel).

But most of the terms of the contract are not like this; they are less conscious, and less clearly spelled out. There are a number of subliminal questions that the reader will be asking of the writer, a few examples of which might be: does s/he know what s/he's talking about? Or, does s/he know where s/he's going? And, is s/he a competent writer?

Reassuring the reader on some of these points is quite easy. If you have to introduce *facts* you need to check them or clarify your position really early. As a simple example, you can certainly write about a fantasy London in which St Paul's Cathedral is next to Buckingham Palace. But you *cannot* write the first 234 pages of a novel in which the fictional London seems to be exactly the same as the material London and then suddenly have a character walking from St Paul's Cathedral to Buckingham Palace in less than one minute. You can write about a planet that rotates in the opposite direction from Earth, but you cannot write about a beach in France where the sun rises in the west – or not without explaining or preparing for this in some way.

Be organized

Similarly, the beginning of a piece of writing sets up certain expectations – you can of course refuse to meet these in ways that challenge the reader, but you cannot just lose your sense of direction and go off somewhere else. If there is a murder and a detective in the opening chapter the reader does have a right to expect that there will be a solution and a murderer will be uncovered somewhere along the line. If the body and the detective are never mentioned again, and the story turns out to be about bird watching in the Norfolk Fens the reader will feel frustrated and unhappy. Successful writers need to know where they are going – with their plot, their characters and their every sentence – and the best way to demonstrate that is to go there, without too many pointless diversions or misleading signposts.

This is a large part of what 'trustworthy' means. A writer needs to write with convincing authority. There is a real link between the word 'author' and the word 'authority'. Look them both up in a good dictionary if you do not know what the link is.

There are a number of subliminal questions that the reader will be asking of the writer

But there is another sort of 'trust' involved in this contract. The sort that answers the last of those questions – is s/he a competent writer? Just as, I hope, you would not let someone who claimed to be 'from the council' in the front door without seeing some authorization, so readers will not let writers into their imaginations without seeing something which assures them that this is the real thing. The 'authorization' (*again note the word*) is writerly competence and that is revealed in the authorial voice.

Competent creative writing does not show up just in decent grammar and no spelling mistakes. It shows up in how the writer manages the material. One clear indication of this is what is called 'point of view'.

POINT OF VIEW

Point of view has acquired a certain mystique recently – so much so that sometimes in creative writing manuals and classes you will see (or hear) it abbreviated to P.O.V. But do not be afraid of it – it is nothing but a useful short hand to describe the whole area of who is telling this story and how.

In a film the issue is much clearer: conventionally, you can only have one camera showing you something at a time. You cannot see both sides of someone's head simultaneously; you cannot see a close-up and a long-range shot at the same moment. If two people who have been together start to walk away from each other, the camera will (eventually) have to follow one of them and therefore not the other. Where the camera is, whom it chooses to follow and the physical distance between the character and the camera *is* the director's, and finally the film's, 'point of view'. The same is just as true in writing.

Look at the following sentences:

He hit her.

Being hit hurt her.

I hit her.

He hit me.

Types of narrator

Here in these four simple sentences we can see the same action from different points of view. The first two come from an 'outside observer'. In the first one the observer is focussing on the 'he' and in the second on the 'she'. In the second two we have an 'involved narrator'; in one case the person doing the hitting and in the other the person being hit. The author can select any of these voices and a great many others as well. Here are some, though by no means all, of the possibilities:

❖ An **outside narrator** who knows everything (every character's thoughts, feelings and actions, and everything that is going on in the outside world). This is usually called the 'omniscient author' or the 'author as God'. It is still probably the most common point of view for novels although not for stories and poems. It is very seldom the point of view of autobiography. This authorial voice uses the 'third person' – he, she and they.

❖ An **outside narrator** who does not know everything. Who, for example, only knows the inner life of one character and sees the world through that character's eyes and actions.

❖ An **involved narrator** who is the central character of the story. This narrator uses the 'first person' – 'I' or 'we'. This is the almost inevitable point of view of a personal memoir or autobiography; it is the probable point of view of a poem and is also increasingly popular in stories, and novels.

❖ An **involved narrator** who is a minor character in the story they tell; who will also use the first person, but may be in a position to be more critical or distant.

What the narrator can do

All these different narrators can do a whole variety of things. For example:

❖ They can use the present or the past tense.

❖ They can acknowledge the existence of the reader. ('Reader, I married him,' says Jane Eyre – an involved narrator of the first type.) Or they can pretend the reader does not exist and just tell the story. *But they will still have a point of view. When writers say, 'She was beautiful' they are establishing themselves as the sort of person who thinks that this sort of appearance is beautiful. That is a point of view, a personal opinion, an angle on the question. Even the most uninvolved narrator in the world has a point of view – simply by choosing to tell this story, in this way, rather than thousands of other possible stories and possible ways.*

❖ An **outside narrator** can take a long shot; stand back from their characters; treat them as though they were 'real' people, and not go deeply into their inner-most secret lives. (This is what most dramatists do.) Or they can create intense close-ups – so that they can report even on the characters' subconscious lives.

Each of these options offers advantages to the writer, but also has real drawbacks. Just as an example, an involved narrator cannot know anything that is being kept secret from him or her. It is worth thinking about these. For instance:

- ❖ An involved narrator, using the present tense, speaks with great emotional immediacy and intimacy. BUT an involved narrator, using the present tense, can only ever be in one place at a time and cannot know anything that is going on elsewhere.

- ❖ An omniscient outside narrator, using the past tense, can manage a complicated plot; and can place the story in a larger context. BUT an omniscient outside narrator, using the past tense, cannot tell any lies or even withhold much information.

There is another sort of limitation too – a limitation of language. For example:

- ❖ An involved narrator who is a child character can only use the words (and thoughts) that a child of that age would have.

- ❖ An outside narrator who acknowledges the existence of the reader has to guess who that reader is, or readers are, and what language will engage them.

Why narrators need to be 'trustworthy'
But the biggest limitation of all is that once you have made that choice you have to stick to it. This is the central proof of competence that the reader is entitled to ask for. Has this writer made a useful choice – and are they accepting and working with the limitations of it? You cannot suddenly give your six-year-old narrator an

understanding of politics; you cannot give your omniscient narrator moments of amnesia; you cannot suddenly imbue your first person involved narrator with the ability to know another person except through their actions and words.

Of course there are ways round almost everything:

❖ You can have more than one narrator.

❖ You can have a first person narrator remembering their childhood, so that they can deploy the language of an adult to describe the experience of a child.

❖ You can have an outside narrator who (like any good film director) varies the angle of the camera – with panning-shots, tracking-shots and close-ups.

And so on. But the rule remains. Readers will notice breaks or inconsistencies in point of view and it will be a big turn off, because they will not find the writer 'trustworthy'.

I hope that I have shown you not just what point of view is but why it is so important.

In addition it is one of the areas over which the thinking (rational) mind of a writer can genuinely take charge. Deciding who will be the narrator of any piece of writing and how they will tell the story is in the realm of your conscious choice. The story or material to be narrated will often be mined out of your subconscious, and the meaning the reader will read into it will always be outside your control. But point of view is the technical skill by which you can, deliberately and thoughtfully, bring the two into the closest possible relationship. So it really is worth working on.

Developing a range of approaches

You cannot think too much about this aspect of the writer's craft. If you can develop and feel comfortable with an extensive range of points of view and technical approaches, you can solve almost all other problems about plot, and pace and meaning, that are likely to come up. And you can also avoid a sort of 'samey-ness' which can make your writing tedious to you, never mind to the reader. I suppose that most of us, as writers, have particular themes and concerns and subject matter. When we write about these we are at our most authentic: we do not avoid repetition by thinking of new things to write about but by finding new ways to write about them.

What you are aiming for here is to feel so confident in writing from various points of view that you can choose the one most suited to the subject you are writing about, just as a tennis player cannot win consistently with only one type of shot: however good her forehand may be, she also needs a powerful backhand and service and a variety of other strokes too. This will enable her to make choices and control her game.

The way to gain that confidence is to practise, to experiment, to be self-aware and self-critical.

Exercise 25 Experiment with a point of view

- Go for a walk. Or undertake some other reasonably straightforward action. (Cook a meal; drive to the shops; get dressed; mow the lawn.)

- Describe this action from your own point of view. If you keep a journal, or did some of the exercises in the *Travelling the way* chapter, you may already have an appropriate piece of writing – if so you may as well use it. It will almost certainly be in the first person and probably in the past tense. It does not matter much if it is not – just adjust the following exercise to what you have actually got.

☞ Read through what you have written and then put it aside.

☞ Write the description again, this time in the third person and the past tense. This is not a grammar exercise – that is why I suggest that you do not copy anything from the first description. Re-create it as though it were new material. Try and visualize it from the outside.

☞ Write the description again, this time in the third person but from the point of view of an observer who is sitting somewhere very high above the character. This narrator will have a much wider view of the whole situation, and will also (for example) see any people from above; the tops of their heads rather than their full face.

☞ Write the description again, this time in the first person but as a person who is not the original 'you'. Imagine someone else you saw on that walk – what did he or she see, feel or think?

☞ Write the description again, this time in the first person, but as though you were talking directly to an imaginary reader. 'Did you notice that man walking down the street?' and so on.

☞ Write the description again as conversation, as though you were telling it to a friend. You can also write in the friend's side of the conversation.

☛ Write the description in as many different ways as you can think of. How might it appear to a Martian on a first visit to Earth? How would a child describe the activity? Write it as a poem. Write it as a newspaper report.

You probably will not want to do all these things in the same writing session: accumulate them gradually. You may find it useful to read the original piece of writing through once at the start of each session, but do not look at it while you are writing the new accounts.

☛ When you have exhausted the possibilities (or you start to feel bored), re-read all of the pieces in a single sitting. Ask yourself if you have completely maintained the various points of view: could this narrator have known or seen these aspects and actions of the central character? Is the choice of vocabulary appropriate to this narrator? What else might the narrator have told us?

☛ Notice how the pieces are different. Think about which you enjoyed writing most and which gives you the fullest sense of the original activity. Record the experience in your notebook.

Different points of view

Sometimes when I am feeling utterly fed up with my own writing I do this exercise in a slightly more absurd way. I try to describe small daily actions from the point of view of the inanimate objects involved. For example, try to describe brushing your teeth from the point of view of the toothbrush; or vacuuming the carpet from the point of view of the carpet; or planting a bulb from the point of view of the bulb. The best way to do this is in the first person with the object as the central character in the story. You can do it in the present tense, or you can have the object remembering the experience during a period of leisure and deploy the past tense.

This version of the exercise obliges you to do a number of profoundly creative things.

❖ First of all you have to observe the action with great accuracy, which involves *real seeing and observing*.

❖ Then you will need to decide or work out what sort of imaginary sensory equipment a toothbrush might have – can it hear the bathroom door opening? Can it see with its bristle end? This involves the skill of *applying your imagination within a very specific framework*.

❖ You will need to invent a voice for your toothbrush, or whatever object you pick. Is it male or female? Clever or stupid? Active or passive? Emotional or practical? This involves really looking at your *language choices*.

❖ You will also find, whether you plan to or not, that the toothbrush has an emotional relationship with its work – it is dutiful; it is happy; it is disgusted. Consider its *character development*.

This is also a great exercise if you have other people to work with. I have often done it with creative writing groups and classes, because it is not just great fun, but is also a very good way of reassuring yourself that you really do have a particular and special experience and 'take' on life – that unique voice we discussed at the very beginning of the book. Here is a terribly ordinary event that most of us perform daily and yet I have never heard two accounts of it that are even remotely alike. The emotional range is huge – I have heard toothbrushes whose experience ranges from the vile to the orgasmic. You will probably learn something about yourself too, but because the context is preposterous it will not feel threatening or disturbing. So in addition to all the other benefits you may well gain some new self-awareness.

I hope I have at least begun to persuade you that, together with language, point of view is *the* central technical tool of strong creative writing. So a couple of points to think about, to practise in your own writing sessions and to remember whenever you have an idea.

- ❖ How you tell your story is a key part of the story you tell. There are lots of ways of telling a story – the more options you think about and the more confident you are when using them, the better your chances of finding the very best one for any particular story.

- ❖ All the choices have advantages and disadvantages – you are not looking for the perfect point of view, you are looking for the best possible one.

- ❖ Point of view is subtle – it is a skill that needs both thought *and* practice.

- ❖ Experimenting with the point of view in a piece of writing is great fun.

CONFLICT AND SUSPENSE

Conflict and suspense are closely related to each other and we often use the terms fairly casually, but they are different and require slightly different techniques.

Conflict (and its resolution) is the stuff of story. It is hard to think of even a very primitive or childish story that does not have any element of conflict. It can be between characters, between the central character and circumstances, *within* the central character, between ideas... but there must be conflict, and if you cannot identify it in your own story you probably have not got a story at all.

Suspense is keeping the reader on their toes, making them want to know, and making them care about what's going to happen next. (Or what happened in the past – though that will be 'next' in terms of their reading experience, because of the linear nature of language.)

Conflict is intrinsic to the story. Suspense is a technique for making the reader interested and excited enough in the conflict to see it through to its resolution.

Scheherazade is the legendary mistress of suspense. In One Thousand and One Nights *the conflict is obvious: if the Sultan gets bored Scheherazade will be executed at dawn. Her technique is based on timing – she must end each night's storytelling at the point when the Sultan's desire to know 'what next?' is greater than his desire to kill her. She has two separate but related problems: first she has to think of a story that offers real conflict, and think of one that is original enough for the Sultan not to be able to guess the ending. And then she has to tell it. Obviously she must not rush the story or it will finish too soon, or the*

Sultan won't have engaged enough with the characters, or understood enough of the dynamics, to care what happens next. But nor must she dawdle on so long with the minutiae and detail that the story does not have a sufficient head of steam to reach a crisis point at the crucial moment, or the Sultan will get so bored that he will stop caring whether or not the characters resolve their conflict.

We can learn a great deal about conflict and suspense from Scheherazade.

Developing your sense of suspense

It is quite difficult within this topic to recommend the sort of specific exercises I have been suggesting in other areas. Conflict, suspense and resolution are always 'whole work' issues. This is as true of the conflict of ideas or images in a short poem (how will the writer bring this to a satisfying resolution in just six more lines?) as it is in the complex plots of an epic novel.

However here are some ideas that may help you develop and sharpen your own sense of suspense.

Think of a horror film, that you remember as being particularly tense. *Psycho* and *The Shining* are two good examples. Watch the film again, critically. Take notes on how the suspense is built up. One of the things that may surprise you is that the excitement does not come from a faster and faster pace – but rather the reverse. From the very beginning of *Psycho* we know that something horrible is going to happen: the music, the situation, even the fact that Alfred Hitchcock directed it, tell us so. Something nasty is going to happen. Then Hitchcock delays and delays over letting us know *what*. Over and over again he seems to be leading us towards an immediate catastrophe, and then he pulls back. By the time Janet Leigh does

Suspense is a technique for making the reader interested and excited enough in the conflict to see it through

159

actually get stabbed in the shower we are both prepared for it and conversely hopeful that this time it will, once again, be all right. In *The Shining* the child rides his tricycle along the corridors of the hotel; one of the longest tracking shots in cinematographic history. At each corner we are geared up for something horrible to happen.

You do not build suspense by rushing into your story, forcing the pace and hurling the reader into an extreme situation. You linger, tantalising them, promising and not quite delivering in whatever way is appropriate to the conflict you are describing. You develop the situation, never repeating yourself, moving inexorably towards climax.

Building up the climax

When you arrive at the climax, however, nothing breaks the suspense more for the readers than to find they suddenly need additional information. You need to be certain that you have provided all the facts (intellectual or emotional) needed to make sense of the situation. A rather crude example would be if you wanted to have a character chased by a bull. You would build up to the moment gradually – describing his or her peaceful walk through the countryside, emphasizing the beauty and wildness of nature for instance, and showing him or her climbing over the fence and so on. Suddenly the bull is charging; the character is terrified, panicked. Now is *not* the moment to write about the red jacket that this character put on that morning. Nor is now a good moment to announce that this character is especially frightened of bulls because his or her mother was killed by one. The jacket, or the psychological past, needs to be well in place before the bull is even suspected.

This business of making sure that the information is already available to the readers is called 'seeding'. As you approach a particularly

In writing, life is pared down to focus intensely on some particular aspect of the whole

important moment of conflict or suspense in your writing you need to
pause and check that you have 'seeded' the climax thoroughly.

Keeping it simple

As I have said in a previous section, real life is littered with coincidence, accident and diversions from 'the plot'. Writing is different – life is pared down to focus intensely on some particular aspect of the whole. Plots will lose suspense if there are so many red herrings, *culs de sac* and irrelevant characters and incidents that the readers lose sight of what the central conflict really is about.

There is a story about a new playwright who went to see his first play in rehearsal. He was appalled to find the director removing line after line of his precious dialogue. Finally, desperate, he said, 'Does that line really have to go? I thought it was rather a good line'. The director replied, 'It is an excellent line - put it in a different play'.

This is an attitude worth developing. So often I have written what I know is a good scene. Yet at the same time I also know that it does not really have anything to do with the conflict I am trying to write about. It used to feel almost impossible to remove it, but now I have learned to think to myself – there, there is the beginning of the next thing I write. And I won't be able to use it if I leave it in here!

This is true even when you are writing something based on a true story – just because an incident really did happen, there is no proof that it belongs in your writing, because writing and real life are fundamentally different. Spurious episodes, true or invented, quickly lay a killer hand on suspense, which is essential.

The climactic scene

Choreograph your climactic scenes very carefully. If you can really visualise *exactly* what is happening, where all the characters are, how

they all react to everything that goes on, what the place looks like, what time of the day and year it is – in short anything and everything – then there is a chance that you will be able to tell it convincingly. Make sure any props are in place and you know where they are. You will not need to tell everything you know, but the writers who know *more* than they need are in a far stronger position than the ones who know less than they need.

Here there really **is** an exercise – it is particularly useful if you are writing an episode that is meant to be full of suspense and conflict and you suddenly find you are getting bored with it all.

Exercise 26 Set the scene for suspense

➪ Draw a diagram or map of the place where the scene is taking place. Fill in all the details, in depth. (Not just 'a tree' but 'an old oak tree, with a scar where it lost a large branch in the 1987 hurricane'.)

➪ List the cast of your scene, again in detail but only the external details, not the emotional or psychological details – what they look like, what they are wearing.

➪ Write the episode as though it were a scene from a film, using only *stage directions* and, if relevant, the actual words of any conversations. Do not include any explanations, motivations or psychological insights at this point.

You may well find that this discipline, which involves fully thinking through the material reality of a situation, brings it to life for you and that the writing of it in whatever form you were originally planning to use – prose or poetry – becomes quite straightforward.

Staying with the characters

Whatever point of view you are using, at moments when you want to create tension and suspense you must stay as close to the characters as possible: show the readers their feelings and thoughts as they feel and think them. These are not the moments to retreat into generalities and abstract truths, however interesting your ideas may be. Don't talk about the nature of fear, love, hope, shopping or anything else – just *show* the characters doing, saying, thinking or feeling whatever it is that these particular individuals would do, say, think and feel in this situation.

There is a temptation to believe that you can make a particular event or feeling more immediate to more people by making it more general – by presenting it as a universal experience. This ought to be true: everyone has experienced some sort of anger for example, so you would think that if you write, 'He was very angry', everyone, however they personally experience their own anger, would understand and feel with the character. This is not, however, true. I am not quite sure why it is not true, but it isn't. Perhaps it is because there is no such thing as 'generalized anger'. There is my anger and your anger and his, her and their anger – and together, as a collection of experiences, we can deduce some general principles of anger. But if you are describing 'anger' in any fictional sense it has to belong to someone. To persuade your readers to identify with your character's anger – or any other feeling – you have to make the experience as physical, specific to the character and present as you can. For example:

'His fists clenched, and although he forced them into his pockets trying to keep calm, his body tilted forward aggressively and a surge of adrenalin darkened his cheeks.'

> ...you have to make the experience as physical, specific to the character and present as you can

163

Everyday conflict

Remember that conflict and suspense can be built around almost anything. You do not need a stabbing in the shower, a major thunderstorm or a wild passion. Most of the conflicts I actually experience are not in this range at all. They tend to revolve around much more mundane and apparently boring issues – shall I buy the economy washing powder, or a more expensive brand name? What will I cook for supper? Shall I read another page of this novel or telephone my friend or get to my desk and write? It is how we resolve these internal conflicts that distinguishes us from each other; so these choices are the stuff of character.

Exercise 27 Write about choice and conflict

☞ Call to mind a tricky *little* choice you had to make recently. Try and remember something where there was a clear choice, with a consequent result, but not an enormously significant one. (Whether to give in to a child's demand for more sweets; what to wear today; whether to accept an invitation you did not want. That kind of choice.)

☞ Make notes in your notebook on everything you can recall about that moment. What the choice was, what were the advantages and disadvantages of all the options; how you felt as you considered the matter; what you chose in the end and how you felt about it immediately afterwards.

☞ Write an account of the episode, maximizing the suspense. Try and immerse yourself fully in the dilemma of the moment. Build up to the decision.

☞ Imagine a person who might have confronted the same choice and made the opposite decision. Write that account too.

☞ Read the two through and compare them. Which has the most detail? In which do you most feel the conflict and the suspense? Which is the most engaging and interesting to read? Why?

Develop a vocabulary of urgency

Think about the *language* you are using. In moments of conflict and suspense we usually experience a sort of urgency, even when the decision does not matter very much. To reflect the experience fully you need a vocabulary of urgency to match that feeling. Re-read the section about register or atmosphere from the chapter on language, and then look at your own account from the previous exercise. Does the vocabulary you have used reflect the feelings you want to excite?

Let's take, as an example, the choice about buying washing powder in the supermarket. By the time you get to the moment of choice you should have made clear what the choices were, so that you can reduce the climax to a dramatic minimum.

'*She took the box of cheaper powder off the shelf and put it in her shopping trolley.*'

This fully describes the action, but it could do so in much more vivid terms.

'*She snatched the white box and hurled it into her shopping trolley.*'

We have cunningly 'seeded' the account so that the 'white box' is already known to be the cheap one; and we allow the readers to supply the knowledge that in supermarkets, washing powder is kept on shelves. Perhaps 'plain white box' would be sharper, particularly if what had attracted her was the more colourful one.

There are perhaps verbs that will more fully illuminate her character or give meaning to her choice:

Took: snatched, grabbed, seized, lifted, pulled, tugged, reached for, heaved.

Put: hurled, placed, shoved, smuggled, dumped *(she's depressed)*, enthroned *(she's triumphant)*.

On the whole, without turning any of these into absolute rules, you will usually find that shorter, simply constructed sentences, active verbs, fewer adjectives and adverbs, and words with hard rather than soft noises in them, add to a mood of decision and action.

VARIETY

No one wants to be bored.

In any piece of writing that is more than a few pages long you should be aiming for a range and variety of, for instance, pace, emotion, tone, voice, point of view, sentence length, space on the page – though not necessarily all of these.

Alice in Wonderland begins:

'Once or twice she had peeped into the book her sister was reading, but it had no pictures or conversations in it, "and what is the use of a book," thought Alice, "without pictures or conversations?"'

At which point Alice falls sound asleep. Older readers may well do so too, if they are confronted with page after page that looks the same, sounds the same, and repeats the same sort of material.

Getting variety into your writing depends mainly on:

❖ an awareness that it is needed.

❖ an alert and creative mind of your own.

❖ the confidence to handle a variety of voices and registers.

You can improve your capacity for all three quite easily:

❖ Notice how much variety there is in things that you like reading. Even the most thrilling adventure stories have calm moments. Even the most tragic and affecting stories have lighter episodes. Dialogue breaks up the page as you look at it, as well as being a slightly different way to present both characters and necessary information. Short paragraphs add pace; longer paragraphs give you breathing space and allow thoughts and ideas to develop. Descriptive writing gives you a break from conflict.

❖ If you are seriously going about trying to see properly and pay attention to what you see, you will almost inevitably find you have a growing alertness to the range and variety of *things*. If you are engaging in a regular attempt to record this myriad of tiny daily events – people and things, speech and emotions – you will find that your mind is becoming more creative and flexible and capable of finding and noticing variety and connection.

❖ If you write regularly and bravely, try out all these and other exercises. Keep on practising the ones you find hardest and pay attention to what you have written. You will probably be quite surprised to discover that you admire the people who can do it more and more *and* you have a growing confidence in your own ability and capacity to handle a wide variety of forms and voices.

Exercise 28 Experiment with variety

☞ Go back and try some of the exercises that you missed out the first time.

☞ Take an exercise, or a piece of writing from your notebook or journal, and try and write it again in a different way. (You might change the point of view; write it as poem; write it as a play; alter the language register – if it was informal re-write it very grandly for example.)

☞ More playfully, try imposing some bizarre language rule on yourself. Write a descriptive passage *without* using one chosen letter – 'E' 'O' and 'T' are the most challenging; write a simple story in rhyming couplets; write something using words of only one syllable – or, more demandingly, using *no* words with only one syllable.

☞ Write nonsense – inventing new words, or misusing existing ones. Try and use punctuation and the shape of the words on the page to make the passage sound and look as though it had meaning even though it doesn't.

☞ Invent an exercise for yourself that obliges you to do something you have not tried before.

If your writing is enjoyable, interesting and exciting for *you* it is far more likely to prove enjoyable, interesting and exciting for other people too. If you are bored by your writing other people will be bored by your writing. Within the framework of a disciplined writing practice, you need to build in variety for yourself, and variety in the writing will follow that. Some days you will want to push your boundaries, emotional or technical; other days you will want to relax more. As you build up a body of work, through the exercises and through everything else you are writing or thinking about, you will have more and more choices about how to use your time. Sometimes it is a good idea to go right back to the beginning and read everything you have written; sometimes it is more useful to take a tiny section of your writing, a couple of sentences or a paragraph may well be enough, and work on trying to make them even better. It is always worth making notes about what you have been doing and how you felt about it.

PERSUASIVE, EVOCATIVE DESCRIPTIONS

I do not think that the students who made this list were really thinking about long, beautifully detailed descriptions of nature of the kind that were popular in the nineteenth century. Before photography was invented people had very little idea of what places might really look like, and their chances of travel were severely restricted: in this context descriptions of place were very important – reading gave people their window on the wider world.

Nowadays much of that job is done better for us by the camera and by travel itself. Nonetheless there are things that the camera cannot do – but writing can. Pictures can only appeal to one sense – the sense of sight. However, we all know that the other senses are crucial

> ...reading gave people their window on the wider world

to our memories, and our emotions: the smell of a particular food cooking can magically transport us, sometimes without consciously understanding it, back through the years. The same is true too of tastes and sounds, and the 'feel' – the texture and touch – of particular things. This sort of descriptive writing is what I believe the students meant by 'evocative'. Evocative means to call something out, or bring forth. Evocative descriptions call up the thing you are writing about very directly to your readers. This skill of evocative writing is not easy, actually, but it is invaluable and worth thinking about and working on. Luckily there is always a good deal of material to practise on. Here is an exercise to get you started:

Exercise 29 Explore your senses

➭ Undertake a simple action that is associated with a strong sense of smell. A very good place to begin is in the kitchen – make a pot of coffee, chop an onion, grate some strong cheese. You might also mow the lawn, arrange some flowers or go to the local public swimming pool.

➭ Concentrate on the smell; watch your own thoughts as you do so. Make notes on what you experience.

➭ Write a short piece about doing this activity without using any visual description at all. Focus only on the smell and your thoughts about the smell, and if you need any additions use the feel of the onion in your hand, the sound of the moving knife (have you noticed before that when you chop onions they squeak?); the taste on your fingers afterwards. Explore all these sensations.

☛ Try this exercise again, focussing on one of the other senses. You will almost certainly need to change the activity: try listening to the very early morning; feeling the way you peel and eat a banana; tasting a curry that is too hot for you.

There is another aspect to creating powerful description. It lies in the word 'persuasive'. You need to write so that the reader is persuaded that he or she is learning something new, from someone who knows. It is not enough to get all your material facts correct and write them down with well-informed precision and authority. Even the most impeccable information can still fail to call up a concrete image of the thing you were trying to describe, whether based in fact or totally imagined.

The reason it is important to work on this aspect of writing, and to get it right, is because one of the great pleasures in reading, indeed one of the most central things that people read *for*, is to have their minds' horizons expanded. They want to be introduced to new places, new things, new worlds. They want to know. We get to know a new place by being there – smelling, tasting, exploring, listening and looking. When people turn to creative writing they are not looking for a guidebook, but for a convincing feeling of being there.

Place and period in writing are a bit like characters in the sense that you need to introduce them to the readers in a similar way. You do not want to begin with a freeze-frame, a static photograph, onto which you then stick the characters and the action. Instead explore the territory through the characters and the action.

Research and the writer

I am a great believer in 'research': I like learning new things myself and I also think that if I am genuinely curious about something then I am more likely to stimulate curiosity in my readers. But research is only a starting point: after that the material has to be absorbed, organized, and written afresh. It has to fit seamlessly into the writing. It must never sound pontifical or lecturing – it must belong within the story.

Exercise 4 from the *Travelling the way* chapter, where you take a small object and describe it, is a good exercise at this point. Now, though, you can add to it by writing about the object from the point of view of a character who is not you. But even more useful for some writers is the following exercise to help you think about combining research with evocative description.

Exercise 30 Change the feel of the material

➩ Interview someone who does a job that you know very little about. Try and find out as much as possible about the daily aspects of the work. (My experience is that if you tell people what you are doing and why they are nearly always delighted to talk about their work.)

➩ Take notes at the time or as soon as possible afterwards.

➩ Write these notes up. Try writing about it as a poem – this will bring you close to the physical experience. Try writing it in the first person – not quoting your subject, but trying to get inside the physical and emotional world of the work. Focus on making the description vivid and personal – even though the person is not you.

If you find this exercise stimulating there are lots of ways you can do it. The Internet makes research very easy. Rather than interviewing an individual, you can find out about the job online. Nor do you have to confine yourself to contemporary jobs. Pick any small, specific area of knowledge that engages you and pursue it. Here are a few ideas to get you going:

Women's fashions in a particular year outside your memory.
Menus in restaurants in cities you have never visited.
Extreme sports.
Bird life in Bulgaria.

Again you want to write up your notes not as though you were a journalist, but so as to explore the associations and sensations and emotions that you discover within the topic. Once you branch out from my little list you will know that there is some reason why you have picked this job, or this research topic, rather than another. Push into the subject until you understand why you chose it. Work that understanding into the piece of writing.

Chapter 6 Making it

Iread recently that by the time a novel was published it had been, on average, through twelve drafts. Even if we can assume that one of those was a final draft to pick up any points that the commissioning editor wanted dealt with, and one of them was a final copy edit, then the average writer has still written a book ten times before it is sold to a publisher.

When a publishing company decides to take on a book, it will be bought and, prior to publication, handled mainly by a single individual usually called the commissioning editor. When he or she is happy with the text, the manuscript will be sent to a copy editor, who fine-tunes the precise details – spelling, punctuation, continuity, fact-checking and so on. Then it goes to the designer (who will have already decided about page size, font and so on) and finally to the printer, who produces a 'proof' – a set of pages exactly as they will look in print. The writer should always get to see and check the proofs for typesetting errors, but you are not really meant to change the text at this stage, so I am not counting this as a draft.

This comes as a surprise to many people. Thrilled by the deep satisfaction of completing a piece of work, they somehow feel that a quick run-through with the spell-check is all that will be needed. Indeed I still encounter romantics who feel that any serious editing will somehow damage their fragile creation, and destroy the originality and inner truth of their work.

They are wrong.

Actually, of course, as soon as you begin to think about what is involved here, it is obvious that these people are most unlikely to be right.

(even) better

In the first place there is the point that I brought up at the very beginning of the book. Before you can write that great work of literature you have to collect the raw materials. In the same way that the initial exercises were the raw materials of future writing, the first draft of a serious piece of writing is the raw material for that specific work. Or to use a slightly different analogy, remember the cook in my opening chapter, who has to go out and buy the ingredients needed for the recipe. In the first draft a writer is doing much what the cook does when she collects the various items from the refrigerator and weighs out the specific quantities into a mixing bowl. If she stops right there you can hardly call it a meal – she has to stir and combine and flavour the mixture, and then she has to cook it.

Creating the first draft

When you create a first draft of something, you will almost certainly do it over a period of time. In your various writing sessions you will have been in an assortment of moods. You will have been in the process of developing the ideas, digging them out through the writing itself. Even if you knew the story before you began, you will almost certainly have discovered new fragments and links and connections. You will have been gleaning more information about the characters during the drafting process. Your authorial voice will probably have shifted about and so will your selection of language. It is quite likely that your initial ideas will have changed, warped by the black hole of writing, which sucks ideas in, transforms them, and then pushes them out as almost unrecognizable words.

You will, almost inevitably, have written a series of fragments which are connected for you through your experience of the process of writing it all down, but may not be connected at all for anyone else. But what you are trying to produce is a complex, dynamic, seamless whole. If you have even managed to get the continuity right – the various characters have the same names, the same appearance and the same biographies throughout – you will have done pretty well.

And there is more to it than this. In the course of writing the work – and living the life that has gone on around that work – you have made a remarkable number of free choices.

Selecting the best words

I once led a workshop in a prison. The young men in the group were all rather talented and certainly had time to give to the process, but on the whole they did not come from highly literary backgrounds. Nonetheless one happy afternoon we found eighty-three different words to describe ways of walking: stroll, march, stride, pace, mince, totter, lounge, gambol . . . We acted them out too and found they had an astonishing precision: in almost every case there was not another word that described exactly that kind of 'walk'. Now, in your first draft you will have used hundreds if not thousands of words. What are the chances that, as you sat there writing, you came up with exactly the right word every single time? We are not thinking at the moment about correct spelling or possibly incorrect words – we are talking about choosing the best possible words.

Exercise 31 Analyze your word choices

➡ Take some large sheets of paper.

➡ At the top of each sheet write a common word: SAY, ANGER, WALK, RED and HAPPY are a good starting selection.

➡ For five or ten minutes write down all the words you can think of that mean approximately the same thing.

➡ Over the next couple of days, keep adding to the lists. (If you can pin them to a wall or keep them somewhere you can see them, this will be helpful. This also makes a good social game: get other people to play it with you, adding their words to your list.)

➡ If you use a word processor, search your first draft for the starter words – or any other words you know you have used frequently.

➡ Compare your use to your list. Is what you have written the most accurate possible word? Have you used this opportunity to insert both subtlety and variety?

You can also think about language the other way round. Some apparently simple words carry a vast range of meanings. Look up the verb 'make' in a good dictionary and you will find an enormously long entry. It is not so much that 'to make' has a long and complicated history, like some words have, but there is a huge list of different uses for this basic and simple word. Here is a small selection of them:

I made a cake.
I made my bed.
I made money.
I made a mistake.
I made him (do it).
I made up (I applied make up).
I made up to him.
I made up my mind.

I made a journey.

I made haste.

I made a face.

I made it happen.

I made him cross.

I made good time.

I made a mess.

I made it (caught the train).

I made it (became famous).

I made do.

I made it up.

I made a friend.

It made a difference.

It made me sick.

We made peace.

We made war.

We made up.

We made music.

We made love.

In addition – and I put this in for my own delight – the word 'poet' is derived from the Greek word ποητεσ (poetes) which means 'maker'.

You may very easily have overused the word 'make' or applied a less than perfectly accurate preposition.

You can make this sort of list with a number of other words (try PUT for example), and it is a good exercise to do so.

The point I am trying to make here is quite simple really – in terms of vocabulary alone it is unlikely that, in the heat of the writing moment, you will always have made the best possible choice.

Other choices

Yet, in a sense, vocabulary is the easiest of the choices you have made. There may be a lot of words for 'walk' but there are not an infinite number. When it comes to ideas, scenes, characters, plots, metaphors, associations and possible interpretations and meanings there are an infinite number of possibilities. You want two characters to meet accidentally: is the scene you have chosen for that to happen the only possible way it could happen? And if not, have you chosen the best possible way for it to happen?

On top of all these choices you need to keep in mind that primarily you are trying to communicate something; something unique and personal to you. We all know that in the most basic, spoken communication things go wrong all the time. Conversation is peppered with phrases like, 'Can you say that again?'; 'I don't get it.'; 'That wasn't what I meant.' and 'You don't understand.' And as we have already seen conversation is supported by a whole range of explanatory gestures and facial expressions. If there is so much room for confusion in casual conversations, how much more likely is it that there will be communication failures in an extended piece of writing, where you are not getting direct feedback from your audience? And yet it matters more that you get it right in writing, because you do not have the chance to go back and explain yourself if someone is baffled.

Remember, we looked at five things that were judged *essential* to readable writing – convincing characters, a clear authorial voice, conflict and suspense, variety, and persuasive descriptions. Then there is a whole list of secondary but important factors as well. It is not very likely, especially in your early attempts, that you will succeed in getting *all* these elements as nearly perfect as you can in a single draft. Bear in mind that when you were learning language the first time, when you learned to speak and understand, it took you about three years and a great many 'drafts' to create an original complex grammatical sentence correctly.

Editing your writing

Redrafting, or self-editing, is as much a part of the creative writing process as the 'inspiration draft' – the first fine flourish, which basically just provides you with something to work on.

The difficulty is that even people who are comfortable accepting that all this is true, often do not really know how to go about the business of editing their own writing. The rest of this chapter will try and show you some techniques for tackling this important task – but once again I need to remind you that there are as many approaches to this task as there are writers. You will need to take from here what is useful to you, dump the rest ruthlessly and work out your own way to do the necessary job.

People, especially when they are new to writing seriously, tend to re-read their writing immediately after they have written it. There is both excitement and reassurance in seeing how much you have written and – at least sometimes – how real and vivid it is. You are fully entitled to that moment of pleasure, but it is not the right time to start editing and rewriting.

There are two reasons for this. The first is that it is surprisingly hard to read something properly when you know word-for-word what it is supposed to say. Most people have a strong tendency to 'read' what they thought they wrote rather than what is actually on the page.

You will nearly always discover that the first 'instant' reading missed quite obvious and blatant errors

When to edit

The second is that when you are writing you 'switch on' a particular part of your brain. If you re-read immediately you are frequently still functioning from inside that creative mind-set. But this part of your brain has a sort of dreamlike quality. It is very good at picking up on deeply buried connections, and on hearing the inner rhythms and sense of a passage. It is naturally sensitive to and affirming of anything creative. However it is not very good at analysing, criticizing, or even noticing inaccuracies, mistakes and errors. If you find this difficult to believe, try it. Wait until you have had a really good writing session and are feeling positive about something you have produced. Read it at once and correct any minor errors (for example spelling mistakes or missing words). Leave the piece for at least twenty-four hours and then read it again. You will nearly always discover that the first instant reading simply missed quite obvious and blatant errors, never mind the subtler nuances of language, form and story.

Take your time

So the first thing to do is to put the writing aside. If you can work on something else for a few sessions, all the better. By all means *think* about the writing – about what you wrote and what you wanted to write and where you think it may have worked; keep notes too on anything more that comes to your mind about the piece of writing, but do not actually read it.

There is no precise length of time that it takes to get yourself ready for the editing part of the work. I have outlined the dangers of trying to do it too soon, but there is also the opposite danger. If you leave it too long you may dissipate the energy that the creative process itself gave to the writing and find that you have lost interest in it. Or you may discover that your attempts to edit cannot recapture the mood of the moment. However I do believe that 'sleeping on it', leaving something at least overnight is crucial. I think that the subconscious needs sleep in order to do its own work – both to shift from one part of the mind to another and to work through the underlying importance and meaning of what you have created. It seems to be a bit like standing dough somewhere warm to rise before you bake the bread, or leaving grape-juice to ferment before you bottle it as wine.

Starting to edit

Nonetheless, let us assume that you have left the writing alone for a while, but now you are ready to go to work on it. The first vital stage is to read what you have actually written properly. There are several possible approaches to this task and I am going to outline three of them

Exercise 32 Become the reader

➤ When you feel ready and have some time to devote to the task read the piece through *as though you were a reader*. This means printing it off if you have written it on a word processor. It probably means leaving your writing space and going to wherever you sit or lie when you read other people's writing. (For some people of course these two happen in the same place, but at any rate try and think of yourself as a reader.)

➤ Read what you have written right through from beginning to end. At this point don't stop to rewrite or even to mark any blatant mistakes – the idea is to read the whole thing as a whole.

➤ As soon as possible after you have read the piece try and make some notes about it. The key questions to ask yourself are:

☞ Is it different in any way from what I thought I had written?

☞ If so, is it more or less interesting than I wanted it to be?

☞ Does it make sense? Is the story coherent? Have I given the reader enough information?

☞ How does it score in relation to the five essential qualities? Are the characters engaging and plausible? Am I, as the narrator, engaging and plausible – is there a clear authorial voice and a sustained point of view? Is there some central conflict and is it tackled in a way that generates and sustains suspense? Is there any variety, or is it all a bit flat and same-ish? Is the background competently presented? Is it forward-moving, complete and sturdy? Is the language vigorous and honest?

☞ How well does it meet other criteria – not just the ones we talked about in the last chapter, but personal ones of your own? Is it the sort of writing you want to write? And if not why not?

☞ If the answer to any of these questions is not to your liking, then ask yourself how you might be able to make your writing better.

The following technique works best with poems or shorter prose pieces. It is a bit cumbersome for a book-length memoir or novel manuscript. You will need a tape recorder.

Exercise 33 Read your work out loud

☞ Read the piece through as I suggested in Exercise 32.

☞ Look back at the notes on p.78 about reading your own work aloud to yourself.

☞ Now record a reading of your written piece. Unless your work is a drama of some kind, try to read fairly neutrally – if you put a great deal of emotion into the reading it may obscure the actual writing.

☞ Reading aloud itself will tell you a good deal about the quality of the writing – because some sentences that look fine at first sight on the page may turn out to be unreadable. Or, as you read, you may see a better version.

☞ Take your notebook and a pen and play the tape back to yourself while you take notes on what you are listening to.

☞ From these notes, ask yourself the sorts of questions I suggested in Exercise 32.

The idea behind the next exercise is to interrogate your text in much the same way as I suggested interrogating your characters in the previous chapter. This is particularly useful if you have a strong motive in relation to the writing style or to the ideas that you want to persuade the reader about.

Exercise 34 Interrogate your text

☞ Read the text through. Put it aside.

☛ In your notebook write the answers to the following sorts of questions:

> What was I trying to achieve in this piece of writing?
> What is it about?
> What is the most important moment?
> What is the strongest line of the writing?
> Who is the central character?
> Why did I choose this point-of-view?
> What is this piece trying to say? Does it say it?
> Does it tell the reader too much, rather than show them what I want them to see through the story and the characters?

☛ Now return to the text and work through it with the questions and answers you have created. Does the writing 'agree' with your answers? Is there a close match between them? If there are differences, do you prefer the actual writing or the idea-of-the-writing?

☛ Take a highlighter pen and mark on the original writing the precise place where each question is most clearly addressed. Notice particularly those questions that you cannot answer from the writing itself. Think about what you could do to provide answers, or to make the question irrelevant.

Whichever way you go about the process of reading what you have written critically, you should end this session with a collection of notes. They will not be corrections or even comments on the page, but separate from the original writing. I myself think that it is a good idea to stop for a while at this stage, and give what you have read and thought a chance to sink in.

Revelations from your writing

At this point you may well find some rather interesting things begin to happen.

You may, for example, discover a completely different sort of writing hidden inside what you wrote – which is, you realize when you see it, what you *really* wanted to write in the first place. You suddenly see that actually this should have been a poem instead of a story; or that it was not really about a fictional character but about something in your own life. Perhaps you start thinking that the story could have gone in a completely different direction, or that the most interesting character is not the person you have focussed on, but someone entirely different, who perhaps only has a very minor role in this version. You took the story off in a false direction. The most positive thing that a first draft can do is to undermine your conscious intentions – and expose your deeper, less conscious ideas and desires.

This is very good news: you have got this top layer out of the way now and have thus cleared a space for the more interesting, more authentic writing to emerge into. When archaeologists begin a new excavation they often have to remove several upper layers of detritus from the site before they can uncover the history beneath. Early drafts can be very like this disciplined approach, provided you are paying good attention to what you are actually writing.

A second and still more pleasurable thing that may happen is that you may surprise yourself. You suddenly find that *this* – this line, this scene, this description, even this whole thing – is very good. You may even experience this response *while simultaneously noticing all the things that are not yet very good*. My own opinion is that you should

> You may discover a completely different sort of writing hidden inside what you wrote

trust these moments. You are, after all, the perfect reader for this particular writer, since you have so many things in common. You would expect to find the writing at least interesting and sometimes impressive. So long as you do not allow that strange excited delight to trick you into believing that you do not need to do any more work you should enjoy the sensation. Take careful note though about exactly what it was that made you feel that way: the ideas, the language, the power of the feelings you have stirred up or the sense of achievement.

Dealing with negative feelings

A distinctly less pleasurable experience you may have is exactly the opposite. Although you felt good while you were writing the piece and were looking forward to re-reading and working on it, suddenly you discover that it is complete, total and catastrophic RUBBISH, fit only for the garbage pail. I am fairly certain that, at least until you are more experienced, you want to be more careful about this response. It may of course be accurate – but all that would mean is that you had been working on the wrong kind of writing, or the particular process you are deploying is not working for you at the moment, *not* that this proves that all your writing (past and future) is doomed to be complete, total and catastrophic rubbish. We all have off-days.

If you have a violently negative feeling when first re-reading something that had felt all right during the earlier writing phase it can be about a number of different aspects of the craft:

❖ You are not writing in a form that really suits you: try something different.

❖ You are not writing in a way that lets you get into your own authentic voice: try some different exercises, or even a different instruction manual; try longer or shorter writing sessions. If you have been using a word processor try longhand (and *vice versa)*.

❖ You aren't listening to your own real concerns, or observations, but are trying 'too hard' to do what you think of as 'proper creative writing' – try writing about your childhood, especially your schooldays. This may well provoke memories that will help you to understand why you don't trust your own perceptions.

It is worth remembering, though, that – as I mentioned in the opening chapter – inside all of us is a rather nasty negative little splinter of identity that does not want us to be as fully creative and free as we could be. I am going to talk about this more in the *Problems* chapter that follows, but for the moment the important thing is to test the feeling against the actual writing. Ask yourself sternly, '*What* is rubbish? What *precisely* is so bad here?' If the answer you seem to get is that it is you as a person that is rubbish, you can be certain that this is something to do with your personality and not with writing at all in the direct sense. It does not have anything at all to do with what you are supposed to be looking at just now. If however it is something specific in the writing – the unconvincing characters or descriptions, the stilted conversation, the cliché-ridden and flat writing, the weakness of the plot, the lack of movement, or anything else – then you know what you have to work on. This can be quite a good moment to go back to the highlighter pen exercise from Chapter 3. Mark anything good in the writing with one colour and anything you want to change in another and see what you have got.

Starting too soon

There are some other interesting phenomena that can appear when you read your own work attentively. On re-reading a first draft you will often suddenly realize that, although the writing is basically sound, you have started it in the wrong place. Most commonly you will find you have started too soon – the reader does not need all this introduction and will be bored before they get to the kernel of the writing. The first time you notice this it can be quite disturbing, but you will soon get used to it because it is a very frequent writing event.

In fact there is a sort of joke about it, especially with poetry and short stories: you write the first draft and then you simply delete the two opening lines (of a poem) or the first two paragraphs (of a short story) and there you are! I have come to believe that I need to write myself into a story. The opening paragraphs of the first draft are just to get me going – finding my way in and establishing the voice. Once that has been accomplished I can get on with the story. These opening lines have nothing to do with the reader at all, and since the lines have done their job of getting the writing started they can be quickly disposed of. The same thing can happen at the end of something too – careful reading tells you that you have let things trickle on, or inserted a completely unnecessary moral or explanation. Or alternatively you have ended too soon – some writers, once they know where the story is going to end up, unconsciously assume that the reader will know this as well. It is remarkable how often one doesn't bother to finish off a piece of writing.

Patterns in your writing

You may also begin to notice patterns in the way you write. That your style improves when the pace is hotter; that you write best at the beginning of a piece, and have difficulty sustaining it; that it takes

> I have come to believe that I need to 'write' myself into a story. The opening paragraphs are just to get me going

you a while to get going, and improves steadily throughout a writing session; that you write best when you are most informal; that writing about nature is disastrous for your personal voice; that the present tense suits you better than the past; and so on. These things are important to notice. On the one hand you may as well know what you are good at and learn to play from your strengths; and on the other hand you need to work especially hard on the things you aren't good at yet, so as to maximize the choices available to you. What you can learn in these early re-reading and editing sessions is more about yourself as a writer – your rhythm, your real interests, your most natural form.

Hints for re-working your writing

Of course, when you have finished all this navel-gazing and analysis you still have to re-work your piece of writing (probably more than once). Now is the time to start scribbling things on the pages of the writing. Here are some hints.

- ❖ **Keep your first draft**. If you are writing directly onto a word processor make a copy of the piece to edit on to, and save one document to your hard disk. Do not make changes to a single original document. This is less important if you are working by hand, or if you are editing by hand onto a printed document, because you will be able to see the original behind any manual alterations you make. You will almost certainly find that you will want to refer to the first draft at some point.

- ❖ **Examine the overall structure.** Think about the structural changes first. (There is no point in labouring over small bits of writing and perfecting the punctuation until you know that you will actually need those sections in the next draft!) Creating a draft structure in note form can be really useful here – you can easily see where you are going to put the valuable writing from the first draft and also become aware of what new material still needs to be added. Then write the whole piece again according to this plan, until it becomes obviously unusable.

❖ **Decide what to keep**. Make notes about which particular lines, sentences or paragraphs you are going to want to keep *in this piece of writing*. If you find you have written fine fragments but they do not happen to belong in this context, copy them carefully into your notebook or other safe place – then they will tempt you less.

❖ **Fill in the details**. Do not get so carried away with your structure that you rush through it too fast. Skimming over a situation will not make it more exciting. Linger on both the old writing and the new writing, digging out all the richness you can find – whether of character, style, or voice. It is always much easier to cut things out if you go too long than to insert new material later.

❖ **Interrogate your characters**. Keep interrogating your characters; keep trying to learn more about them. (They should be becoming friends by this stage – even if they are the bad guys.) Keep them moving about, rather than freeze-framing them while you tell the reader something about them. Think of new things for them to do (remember that *saying* is one form of *doing* in this context).

❖ **Show, don't tell**. Pick away at any sentences that are *telling* the reader what they should think or feel. See if you can find a way of *showing* the reader instead.

❖ **Avoid sweeping statements**. Look very carefully at any sweeping generalizations or abstractions that may have crept into the writing. Unless you happen to be a nineteenth-century novelist with strong religious convictions take them out. This is especially important at the end of a piece (poetry or prose). Writers have a rather patronizing tendency to make sure the reader 'gets it'. Just in case they haven't, too many writers spell out what the story was about in high-minded and long-winded terms. If the reader cannot grasp your 'moral' from reading the writing, the fault is not theirs but yours.

❖ **Be aware of language idiosyncrasies**. Most writers have personal quirks of language – it is these indeed that make up a significant part of a writer's individual style. (Some of mine are writing in triplets without a conjunction before the last of three phrases; beginning sentences with 'and'; and using proper nouns where most people would use pronouns.) Try and identify what yours are and then watch them appear. If they get out of hand and start clambering all over your writing it will look affected and be irritating. You probably do not want to eliminate them, but you do want to be aware of them so that you can control them.

❖ **Pay attention**. Be aware of each sentence, each phrase, if necessary. If the writing starts to feel somehow flat and dull, try 'inspecting' it. Look at the following general rules and see if you are breaking them. (Be careful though, there are of course always exceptions.)

❖ **Strong verbs are healthy**.

❖ **Adverbs are unhealthy** – the fewer the better. Adverbs will seldom bolster weak verbs. ('She went slowly' v. 'she dawdled'. Which feels more vivid?)

❖ **Always prefer active to passive verbs, where possible**.

❖ **Avoid repeating individual words or turns of phrase**. This rule is untrue more often than most: reiteration can be very effective in both poetry and prose – see the Authorised Version of the Bible. But if you mean to and want to, it is a very different matter from finding that you have deployed the same word five times in two pages.

❖ **Be careful about adjectives**: the fewer and more precise the better. I have a bad tendency towards too many adjectives and so I now underline every adjective I have used in a first draft and ask each one to justify itself. Remember, if you are finding all this a bit difficult to follow you might like to look at the grammatical glossary at the back of the book.

❖ **Appreciate the effect of punctuation**. Finally, do not neglect your punctuation – it is one of the most valuable tools of the trade. Before the fourth century CE when people learned to read silently, without moving their lips, there was no punctuation in writing. *Therewerenobreaksbetweenwordseither,* just as there are none in speech. Because readers had to speak, their breathing made the flow of the words intelligible. Once people could read without speaking they discovered that it was well-nigh impossible to make sense of written language. Punctuation was the brilliant idea that made modern reading possible. The different punctuation marks represent the original breathing and pausing on the page. If you don't breath you die; if you don't punctuate your writing dies.

Punctuation (like spelling) is highly 'conventional': there is no moral right or wrong, but there is a general agreement, and that agreement simplifies the combined task of the writer and the reader – extracting sense and meaning from all those little scratches on paper. This gives writers, who understand the rules of the game, a great deal of control over how their writing will be read. So, when you come to edit your own text think about the punctuation as well as all the other details. I have two small hints though:

❖ Overuse of the exclamation mark [!] will not make your writing more vivid or tense. It will not make lines funny which were not funny without an exclamation mark. Except in conversation, and even there use extreme moderation, the exclamation mark should be avoided.

❖ Parentheses or brackets ( ) should also be avoided in fiction. I am not entirely clear why this should be so, but brackets seem to undermine the trustworthiness of the authorial voice. They somehow imply that the writer has failed to organize their thoughts and ideas properly.

After you have edited and rewritten your piece of writing, put it aside for a day or so and then do it again. And again.

And again? Eventually you will reach a point where you become aware that rather than getting better and stronger with each rewrite, the reverse is happening. The poor old piece of writing is falling asleep from exhaustion. Take the draft from the rewrite before that happened and treat it, for the time being at least, as the final, finished 'top copy'.

Congratulations.

Chapter 7 Problems

By now I hope you are building up a regular writing practice, which at least some of the time gives you real pleasure. I hope, too, that you are also building up a body of work. Much of it will probably still be in a rather misty condition – notes and scrappy journal entries and fragments of this and that – but out of all this you should be beginning to have a sense of what you might be writing and how to go about it.

I hope, too, that you are feeling both more confident and more humble about the whole business. More confident because you have a clearer view of what writing might entail and a growing gut understanding that none of it is 'too difficult' for you. And more humble because you should also be aware of just how much hard work it takes to write something that pleases you as a writer – and how much more work it takes to write something that pleases you as a reader. In this context though, 'humble' should also mean self-tolerant; you don't have to beat yourself up because you know all too well that Shakespeare (and quite a few other writers) are better at this than you are.

So far, so good.

But it will not always be 'so good.' Things do go wrong. The flow of the writing dries up; you find your writing sessions difficult, even boring. Life becomes a bit overwhelming and you miss a couple of sessions and then it is hard to get started again. The writing doesn't seem to get better as fast as it did in the beginning.

Again, you could be producing excellent notes but somehow they never turn into anything finished. You can feel your promising opening winding down and the energy you started with gradually subsiding. Everything you write seems vapid – or worse the writing

It will not always be 'so good'. Things do go wrong

is fine and strong, but doesn't seem to be saying anything worth saying. You know you have something worth saying, you even know what it is, but each time you look at what you write you know that you have 'lost the plot'. You realise that a novel is nearly 100,000 words long and you can only write a maximum of about 300 words at a time and about half of those are useless anyway. You recognize that your best poem is derivative, incomprehensible and riddled with clichés – and what is more it simply isn't finished yet.

It all feels a bit scary and too close to the bone.

It all feels a bit pointless and a waste of your time.

It all feels a bit too difficult and you doubt you are up to it.

In fact, you haven't even made a single note in your notebook for the last month and yet you *still* know that you want to write.

In this chapter I want to look at some of the things that go wrong and some of the ways you can try to get them to go right.

All in the mind?

Some of the reasons why we fail to achieve the things that we consciously believe we want to achieve, or even why we do not do the things that we know give us pleasure when we do them are, of course, psychological. We all live with conflicting desires, particularly around issues of pleasure and power. These have nothing to do with writing *per se* – and are outside the remit of this book. If your desire to write and your failure to do so spring from this sort of internal conflict and this is causing you real distress then you must seek your healing elsewhere. I am not qualified to address those issues, and deeply believe that unqualified interference in such matters – especially in a book where there is no face-to-face contact or personal commitment – is more likely to do harm than good. I am, of course, very conscious of the fact that writing is advocated as a therapy and indeed know that it can help people enormously. But this is a craft book not a therapy book. The issues I am going to talk through in this chapter are practical and pragmatic, and are to do with the problems of writing not of living. If you need or want to probe the latter, you need to find support of a different kind.

Why have you stopped writing?

Grinding to a halt is the most common version of 'something going wrong'. It happens everywhere, all the time. Evening classes, for example, have a built-in expectation that many people there at the first class will not be there at the last class. The drop out rate is even higher when people are trying to study something on their own. People make New Year's resolutions, buy equipment, enrol on courses and purchase training manuals with genuine and heartfelt commitment – and then let the whole thing slide away.

There is a tendency to berate ourselves for this, to assume that it is simply laziness or lack of commitment, and that this is somehow 'bad.' We feel guilty or angry with ourselves, and – because these are not very agreeable feelings – we get increasingly negative about the whole project and are far less likely to wrestle with the problem and so solve it. This is not very helpful. I think it is important to try and find out *why* we have stopped doing some activity we thought we would like to do, because different causes require different cures.

Perhaps you have stopped writing for a very simple reason: it did not deliver what you hoped it would. You thought you wanted to do some writing but now you have tried it, you have learned that quite honestly you don't. This happens quite often with writing, because at first sight writing seems to be the 'easiest' of the art forms to get into. And it is certainly the cheapest. If your underlying desire was to learn some creative skills, and express some creative aspects of your personality – then maybe writing is not the best way for you to do this. Getting as far as finding this out is an enormous step forward, because now you will have opened up the space to explore alternatives – music, the visual arts, garden design. All that energy that was tied up in thinking 'I want to do some writing' is now liberated. Use your journal or notebook to explore more precisely what it is you want to do.

Exercise 35 Discover your creative direction

☞ Go to an art gallery or museum – ideally a fairly large one, and one that displays a range of different sorts of paintings from different periods of history.

☞ Walk around quite steadily – I mean look properly but do not linger over any particular painting.

☞ When you have had enough (two hours is *more* than enough if you are not used to looking at visual art).

☞ Sit down, away from the pictures, and try and remember two or three of them that made some impact on you.

☞ Go back and look at just those ones.

☞ Ask yourself if you are at all attracted to creating such things.

You can use this, or a similar exercise, with other media of course.

Remember – you do not have to write at all. There is no obligation to commit your thoughts, ideas, experiences, dreams or stories to paper. If you choose not to do so that is a perfectly proper and honest choice.

One reason why writing is not satisfying to some people is because it is essentially such a solitary act. You may well want to express yourself in ways that carry meaning beyond the purely private. But if you think about it, writing is a slightly odd way to go about this – because it forces you into solitude and privacy. Quite simply it may not suit *you* to lock yourself away from the world for several hours a week in order to communicate *with* or *to* the world. This seems entirely reasonable to me. I suggest you look for an art form with a more sociable practice.

If, as you read this, you sense that this might indeed be your difficulty but you aren't certain, it can be a good idea to try a creative writing group or class, and see if sharing your work with other people re-establishes your sense of purpose. Especially at the beginning of any learning experience, a community can provide real ballast and support.

However, you may be somehow and somewhere quietly confident that you do want to push on with this writing business. What you are facing is the first major technical challenge of your writing journey. In the rest of this chapter I am going to look at some of these challenges: it is up to you to decide which one is the most likely cause of your problems and then experiment with my practical suggestions. They are just things that have worked for me, or for my students and colleagues. I very much hope you will not need all these ideas at any one time!

Boredom or laziness

A couple of the most common reasons why writing falters is boredom and/or laziness.

The two are surprisingly closely connected. Since it cannot actually be boring to express your thoughts in a new way, if you feel you are bored make very sure that this is not a tasteful excuse for being too idle to get down to work. Your writing muscles will very quickly grow weak and flabby. You need to exercise them.

Exercise 36 Getting restarted

➤ Leave the particular piece you are finding stressful. Tell yourself that you may not work on it any more until you have written something else at least 1,000 words long.

➤ *(Sometimes just forbidding yourself to tackle a particular task transforms the whole situation. It becomes the only and most demanding thing that you really have to do. Problem solved!)*

➤ Make your writing sessions five or ten minutes *shorter* than usual. This puts a little, but not unbearable, pressure on you to get on with it.

➤ Go back to the *Travelling the way* chapter and try some of those exercises again. Pick the ones that seem to have the least to do with the writing you are struggling with.

If you have worked those exercises to death here are a few new ones. They are meant to be stimulating. The idea is to re-engage your imagination and sensitivity with the issue of language and writing. Don't take them too seriously. Whatever anyone says about all the necessary *angst* and grief of the artistic process, it is in fact extremely difficult to write if you are stressed, depressed, or sluggish.

Exercise 37 Write about a colour

➡ Go to a large DIY shop and select some colour cards – those bits of paper that have samples of paint colours on them. Best of all for this exercise are the ones for the mix-to-order paints, so that there are a good number of very similar colours and tones on a single card.

➡ If these colours already have names ('Caribbean Romance', 'Desert Dawn' and so on) obliterate them with a heavy black felt-tip, so they don't distract you.

➡ Look at each colour individually and with attention. Try and think of something you have seen or imagined which is that exact colour. Write one sentence about that object; or about anything else you associate that colour with.

Exercise 38 Write about an emotion

➡ Select one emotion – love, anger, jealousy, loss, joy.

➡ Describe that emotion in terms of each of the five senses: sight, sound, taste, feel and smell. ('Joy smells of springtime', 'jealousy tastes like old copper coins'.) For each emotion you tackle you should therefore end up with five concrete images – five sentences or ideas.

➡ Edit these five images into a poem, by changing the order and, if necessary, individual words.

☛ Advanced version: If you find this stimulating, you can try it with any abstract noun – freedom, isolation, punctuality. This is more difficult because the connection between emotions and senses is closer than the relationship between truly abstract nouns and sensory perception.

Exercise 39 Write about your childhood

☛ Recall an incident from your childhood.

☛ Make some rough notes recording the facts as you remember them. (Feelings are part of the facts.)

☛ Write about the episode from the point of view of a child of the age you were then.

☛ Write it again from the point of view of an adult who was there at the time.

☛ Think about how different their concerns and interests were. Have you been fair to both voices?

Exercise 40 Write a haiku

☛ Go for a walk. (You can do this exercise without moving actually, just by looking around the room you are in, but it is more fun to get out.)

☛ Look at one thing completely. In a sense the smaller the better. A leaf, a blade of grass, one square inch of pavement, the door handle of car. Anything will do. But *really* look.

➤ When you get home, write down everything you can think of about the object.

➤ Write a *haiku* about it. This will make your use of language as concentrated as your experience of looking.

A haiku is a classic Japanese poetry form. It has seventeen syllables, divided into three lines of five, seven and five syllables. It should describe an immediate and personal experience and it should contain at least one 'season word' – a word that reveals what time of year the poem is set in. (It does not have to be 'spring' or 'winter'; it can be an indirect reference, a one-word metaphor, like 'cherry blossom' or 'snow'.) If you find this form interesting there are a good many websites that will give you examples and more detailed instructions.

The best way to deal with the feeling of inertia is to amuse yourself. Have fun. Try something new and different. Challenge yourself with something difficult. Write anything.

Above all keep writing. It is you who wants to do this ridiculous thing. No one else is going to make you write; probably at this point no one else cares whether or not you are going to write. At the very worst, just sit. Go to your writing place and sit there, pen in hand, and wait. That will probably be so boring that you will write something just to get away from yourself.

Avoiding self-censorship

At this stage in your writing journey, another very common cause of the writing drying up is **self-censorship.**

This requires a more intellectual, proactive response from the would-be writer. First of all you simply have to accept that all of us have a strong internal censor, which actively tries to stop us 'telling the truth', or writing authentically from the centre of ourselves, which is the only place where we can hope to find our own unique and valuable voice. You will need to do daily battle with the restrictions this disagreeable internal character tries to set. What you need to do is recognize the reality of this censorship and learn to watch out for its highly subtle wiles. There are however some solidly practical things you can do.

To start with, you must refuse to be afraid of writing something that seems to be rubbish. It may be rubbish, in which case it needs to be cleared out of the way so you can discover what sort of writing is underneath, but it is just as likely to be gold dust and you won't know that until you have written it. Just accept that you do not yet know what this writing is and keep on going.

Writers and the law

A particularly annoying device of this internal censor is to try and persuade you that what you are writing is somehow criminal, 'against the law'. The best defence against this particular version of internal censorship is to be clear about what the law really says.

We pride ourselves on the freedom of speech that we enjoy. Of course this is relative: different countries have different freedoms. The legal inhibitions in the UK fall into a number of categories, most of which you could not breach even if you tried. There are laws controlling and restricting the publication of obscenity, blasphemy (only against Christianity) and racism. There are moves to extend these laws to cover other discriminatory categories. There are also laws relating to national security, like the Official Secrets Act.

There are injunctions – court orders, issued by a judge in response to a direct application, which prevent the publication of individual

The best way to deal with the feeling of inertia is to amuse yourself. Have fun

articles or specific information. There are also some more long-term and general injunctions, like the one against publishing the names of defendants in criminal cases if they are under-age. And finally in this group there are the peculiarly British *sub judice* rulings, which rigorously limit what you can report about people between the time they are charged with a criminal offence and the final court judgement.

There are rules of professional confidentiality. These prevent you from giving away information about your clients. For journalists there are some specific semi-voluntary rules of behaviour, which are policed by the Press Council.

Of further interest to writers are the laws that state that you may not publish or profit from copyright material belonging to another writer. Nor may you publish untrue damaging statements about other people; this is called libel. Note, though, that it is not illegal to publish untrue statements that are not damaging, or true statements that are damaging. There has to be an element of 'wilfulness' in the untruth – this explains the little paragraph at the beginning of many novels claiming that all the characters are fictional. You cannot under any circumstances libel people who are dead – even if their relatives are alive and offended.

Look through these rules carefully. None of them are likely to have much effect on your writing. Remember it is publication (rather than the writing itself), which constitutes the crime. When you have a publisher they will be highly sensitive and perfectly well-informed about possible illegalities. Write what you want to write and let them deal with any problems.

Writers and their 'internal law'

The real and important message here is not to confuse any woolly misunderstandings of the law with your own internal censor. It is very seldom really the law or the neighbours that get in the way of honest writing. It is you.

When I find myself undermining my own writing in this way, I have a little game I play. Whenever something feels inhibiting, I imagine a whole cast of characters being activated; they are parts of me and I have now given them quasi-visual identities so that I can negotiate with them. Among them are:

The writer. *The writer is not amoral, but her moral duty is only to the writing. She is faithful to the task of doing this as well as possible – and in that cause is fairly ruthless. She has very little sympathy with any of the other characters. She wears spectacles.*

The little girl. *Writing gives you power. The little girl suddenly discovers this power. It is very tempting to 'pay back' all the hurt feelings of a child in your writing. The little girl is pretty anarchic and constantly urges the writer to go too far. Her judgement is uncertain and her literary skills nil. She is fierce and courageous, but she likes to claim the privilege of 'artistic integrity' to exact a low revenge. She has scabs on her knees and long plaits in her hair.*

The angel. *This character wants life to be happy and wants other people to feel good. Recently it has become fashionable to despise the angel, and see any tendency to be kind to those around us as somehow cowardly and dishonest. I don't agree – I think that writing, imagining new worlds and communicating them to others entirely through language requires a real generosity of spirit. Love and loyalty are perfectly proper human feelings and need to be acknowledged and given space. Mine is rather a plump angel, with pinkish wings.*

The demon of shame. *There is a problem about the angel though. The demon of shame is very clever at disguising itself as the angel. The demon will often try and persuade you that you are being nice to someone, when in fact you are only protecting yourself from the faintly embarrassing feelings that may come when you are writing authentically. The demon carries a short sharp stick for prodding me with.*

The professor. *The professor is a perfectionist. His idea is that you cannot get on with the writing until you have done lots more research. You need to know everything and must stop writing freely while you bone up on an obscure fact that you may need later. He wears an egg-stained tie and has a row of pens in his top pocket.*

My device is to bring these characters together and make them talk to each other. I write their conversations down, as though it were a mini-play script. One point about this exercise is that you will be analysing the problem. The other point is that you will be doing some actual creative writing. Since the difficulty was that you were stuck or had ground to a halt, you will be well on your way to a resolution. The imaginative element of the exercise makes it a great deal easier than brutal self-criticism and blame, and it is a great deal more fun to think about as a result, too.

The need to know yourself

The better you know yourself, the better you will be at writing. Equally, writing anything attentively teaches you about yourself. It is extremely difficult to write well while suppressing things you know to be true. I am not sure quite why this is the case, but there is a fairly widespread agreement that although you may not have to write everything, you do have to acknowledge, to yourself at least, what is going on inside. The time to tackle this is in a first draft. Silence all the voices now and just write. The point is you can always destroy that first draft (or better still keep it under lock and key). The idea is not to let the censor get in the way of this initial, personal and private exploration.

Once something is out there, on the page, separate from you, you may well find it is not as scary or hideous as you feared. You may of course find that it is worse. But once it is written down, however secretly, it will probably stop getting in the way.

Trying too hard

Another common reason for losing your way is trying too hard. Here I do not mean working too hard, I mean trying for an effect that is not your own. Being too clever or too literary are the most common forms of this disease. Instead of writing down what you actually see or actually feel, you slip into writing down what-you-believe-a-writer-would-see-or-feel.

This is where cliché comes from – a cliché is a phrase that was so accurate when it was first used that it stuck in people's minds, and has now been used so often that instead of helping a reader to see it gets in the way of any real seeing. It sounds real to you as you write, but in fact is not true to your experience.

This is also where preposterous distortions of word-order come from, usually in poetry. Would-be poets want to sound like what they imagine are 'real' poets: one cheap way to do this is write, 'Unto the house came he' instead of 'he came to the house'.

Essentially if you are trying too hard, both the intelligent reader in you and your own authentic writing voice get so bored that they tune out and refuse to co-operate any more. There are two treatments for this disease, because there are two sources of infection:

The better you know yourself, the better you will be at writing

209

❖ **A loss of confidence**. You stop believing that your imagination has any validity or worth. You cease to recognize that your voice is unique and that its uniqueness is your only gift to the world as far as writing goes. The treatment is to re-read the opening chapter of this book; and to look back at your journals and notebooks from before you got sucked into this bog of affectation and worry.

❖ **A shortage of decent models**. You simply do not read enough to discover just how many authentic and moving ways of writing there are. Lot of poets do not distort syntax. Lots of writing does not use clichés or any of the other little tricks you keep trying to shove in between your experience and the reader's experience. The treatment is to read more, to read lots. In particular read something you have never read before. Try reading as much contemporary poetry as possible, because there – in its published form – you will encounter the hundreds of struggles to establish an independent voice more acutely demonstrated (because each poem is likely to be quite short) than anywhere else.

You may need to try both of these to see what works for you.

Coping with difficult writing

There is also another rather different experience of struggling, of 'trying too hard' and feeling you are getting nowhere. It is possible that what you are trying to do is, in fact, genuinely difficult. Either mentally or emotionally, it is demanding more resources than you are able to give it at this time. The tension between the struggles to write whatever it is, and the failure of your own capacity to sustain the scale of the work can lead to a sort of despair. This is without question the most challenging version of 'grinding to a halt'. It is also – though it probably does not feel like it at the time – the most exciting too.

If you have considered all the other options then there are a few strategies that may help here:

❖ Build up your writing muscle by writing other things for a while – journals, exercises, notes, even other full sized projects. Think of this as marathon training – many marathon runners run a half-marathon or other long-distance race, as well as daily workouts and general training, as a way of getting themselves fit for the Big One.

❖ Break the work into more manageable segments. Write some of the more difficult passages as shorter independent pieces; do not worry about fitting them together until you feel you have solved all the separate pieces of the puzzle. Pick away at it bit by bit.

❖ Take this year's holiday as a writing retreat. Give yourself the time and space to do the sort of writing that you cannot reasonably fit into your daily life. *There are places, which are actually designed as writing retreats. There are also all sorts of holidays you can take where the rest of your household can be out doing something in the daytime while you wrestle with the writing. It can be nice to have something else to relax with in the evening.* It is surprising how often a very concentrated spell of work will solve a writing problem that felt intractable in the context of one's daily life.

Lack of focus

Not everyone who feels that something is going wrong in their writing experiences this as 'grinding to a halt' or 'drying up'. Some people have exactly the opposite problem: a sense of being 'all over the place'.

You really enjoy the exercises. You are never at a loss for things to write – indeed you are frequently interrupted while doing other things by a real desire to be in your writing place scribbling away.

You start on a number of projects, many of them clearly unrelated to each other. You are producing, for instance, a regular stream of short poems; you are also generating a plot for a novel; you have two or three short stories on the go, and now suddenly you have become intrigued by radio drama and find yourself, inside your head, experimenting with various interesting possible scenes.

Nonetheless none of this seems to be going anywhere. You cannot develop a consistent voice, get anything finished, or even link the assorted fragments together in your mind. (A particularly frustrating form of this is when you set out thinking that you know exactly what it is that you want to do, and find that you want to work on everything except that original inspiration.)

This experience is very common. In some cases, it may be a rather subtle form of one of the problems I have already raised:

❖ You are avoiding the hard work of pushing a writing project to some conclusion, and are covering up this laziness by superficial energy.

❖ You are self-censoring by being so busy that you cannot get to the heart of any single piece of writing.

❖ You are trying too hard, by maniacally spinning endless webs in the hope of catching the real writer somewhere along the way.

Yet, when you go back to the work, despite your irritation with yourself, it all feels somehow sound and satisfying as far as it goes, and the act of writing itself has an almost addictive quality.

Finding your form

If you are very new to the creative writing journey then the most likely problem is that you have not yet found the form or subject matter that is truly suited to your authentic voice. Keep on thrashing around, keep on trying things out, keep on writing, exploring your craft, learning new tricks of the trade. At the same time be alert for something to click into place. If you think that this may be your problem then one thing that is essential is that you read a lot – not so much in quantity but in range. There is a very good chance that one day you will be reading something quite unexpected and you will find yourself thinking either 'I could do that, but do it better' or, the same thing more negatively, 'I wouldn't do that, I would do...'. You will by now be in first-class training and ready to run with whatever the real idea turns out to be. Relax and enjoy yourself while you find out.

If, on the other hand, this has been going on for some time – perhaps this is the nineteenth such book you have bought (and even worked through) and you have been a member of various writing groups and classes and gone off on residential courses – you need to look at your process and try and see where exactly things are coming unstuck. There are a number of possibilities:

❖ **The wrong sort of humility**. You still are not fully convinced that you have something worth saying. Everything you try feels dull and floppy, and you try more and more things in the vague hope that you will stumble on your own voice. Re-read the opening chapter of this book to reassure yourself and then take a grip. This is the moment for a little self-discipline. Tell yourself you are not allowed to tackle a new subject until you have written the whole of this one. It doesn't have to be a work of genius: it just has to be written through to the end.

❖ **The wrong sort of arrogance**. You think you can do anything and everything. This may be true but first you have to do something – remember there is no great writing 'in your head'. All great writing is on the page – put it there.

❖ **A specific technical problem**. (Your characters feel dead; your plot is stupid; your poetry is banal.) You are writing in circles in the hope of dodging this weakness. Instead, tackle it head-on. If there is not a clear description of how to challenge yourself on a particular aspect of your writing in *this* book, look in some other books, or at one of the writing schools on the web.

❖ **Fear**. You are trying to avoid your real subject matter, and generating lots of other writing as a displacement activity. The creative part of you is pretty unsympathetic to such tricks, and refuses to be satisfied. Try Exercise 3 on p. 34 from the *Travelling the way* chapter – or any other technique you can think of that encourages you to write in the least self-conscious way possible. Try this for three or four consecutive writing sessions, and then look at what you have written and see if you can get any clues.

Finding the problem area

Another way of addressing this unsatisfying sense of being stuck is to look, not at yourself, but at the process of the writing. Try and find out *where* – at which point in the process – the writing is going awry. There are really only three choices – the beginning, the middle or the end.

Beginnings. For me, this is the big problem. I cannot bear to start a new piece of work. I generate a lot of writing around the planned piece without ever properly getting on with the business of starting. I have learned that this is because until I commit myself by writing the first real sentence down, I can fool myself that this time it will be perfect. Writing a single sentence shifts it from the ideal writing in my head, to the actual (flawed but real) writing on the page.

I have found ways of tricking myself. For example, I normally write on a word processor but I have learned to start a big project in longhand, usually on scraps of paper and the backs of envelopes. This feels far less formal and official – part of me can pretend I haven't actually started. I have also learned not to start at what I know is the beginning, but somewhere in the middle. Since starting is the difficult thing I move the earliest phase of the writing away from the problem zone so it feels less alarming.

❖ I present myself with rigorous deadlines.

❖ I promise myself treats, when I have written a decent amount of the text.

I seldom need these rewards because once I get started I can be very quickly absorbed into the writing and forget that after 500 words I was allowed to have a chocolate bar or whatever.

These sorts of tactics look a bit childish written down like this *and they are*, but they do work for me. Experiment with what works for you.

Middles. Writing the whole of something – whatever it is, even a haiku – is very hard work. If you are a writer who finds starting easy, it is much more comfortable to write the beginnings of lots of things, rather than the middle of one.

There is also a temptation to put everything that interests you into the opening of the work, which means that the middle feels dreary and dull.

Then there is the danger that, as you start to feel a bit bored by it, you hurry things up too much – then the writing inevitably thins out and genuinely becomes flatter and less exciting. Then you are bored by it – you get into a loop and it is hard to break out again.

My first bit of advice will sound hopeless, but it is worth trying. Slow down. Go back to the moment when you decided to rush off and try something else. Look at what you were writing at that moment – *now write it again*. Try and make it twice as long as it was the first time, choreograph it with detailed care. Make notes and then instate the material from the notes into the middle of the passage. Try writing it in a slightly different style, from a different point of view, or even in a different form. Luxuriate in the writing. Make expanding *this* piece of writing become whatever it was you hoped to gain from the other piece of writing you were rushing off to do.

A particular form of this boredom is the inability to think of anything new to do with the writing, and particularly with the characters. Writers have a real advantage over other artists – our outlay (except for time) is so small that we can waste it shamelessly. Take the plot somewhere else: kill off all the characters in a

> Look at what you were writing at that moment — and write it again

devastating earthquake; have them abducted by aliens (unless of course you are writing about earthquakes or aliens, in which case taking all the characters to a formal tea party with cucumber sandwiches will be an equivalent).

I once spent two days of work getting my whole cast into a car and spinning it off a cliff – everyone died. Then I tore this up and went back to what was really going on for them. However, I had seen them all in a different context, learned some new things about them and realized why the plot I was working on was better for the reader and for me than all this improbable melodrama. Here I went with the impulse to write something different, but channelled it deliberately back into the work I was meant to be engaged in.

Another well-tried technique for keeping going in the middle of a longer piece of work is to start each session by reading the previous few pages, not to correct them but to allow the story itself to impel you into the next few pages. The fundamental human desire for a story that I spoke about earlier may kick in and demand that you press on. If however you are a perfectionist this may not work: you may feel so compelled to start correcting and rewriting that the 'what-next?' mechanism of basic story does not get a chance to operate. So treat this method experimentally – it is not offered as a magic spell. If it does not help you, forget it.

Endings. Ending anything is tricky – this is a fact of life. All endings have at least a distant note of defeat. If you have enjoyed writing something, ending it can be depressing. If it is fiction you will probably have come to know your characters better than anyone you have known in real life – in a sense that is the point of fictional characters. To close down their lives forever can be hard. Even with forms of writing that are more formally structured, your work will be something you have engaged with for a while, put a lot of yourself into and, almost certainly, have great hopes for. It is difficult not to dribble on, never quite resolving everything. Either you think of just-one-more scene or you keep on rewriting and changing things long after this is making the writing any better.

I have a novelist friend who, when he finds it difficult to let go, sets himself the task of writing a short story about one of the characters; set about twenty years into the future. He finds this an invaluable way of marking the end of the process.

There is another reason why admitting you have finished something (or even could finish it if you were not suffering from this particular kind of being-stuck) is hard. Once you have finished it you will have to take the risk of finding out if other people like it. You will have to stand up and be counted. So it is very tempting not to acknowledge that you have finished, because while it is still unfinished there is a chance that it just might turn into a work of genius, and in any case you don't have to find out.

Read or dead?

Of course, the reality is that you don't have to find out anyway. You can finish it and then throw it on the town rubbish dump, or lock it up in a bottom drawer. Some people will tell you that they don't want to get published, that they write for their own satisfaction and they would not want anyone to see it ever. I never quite believe them. I think that part of the desire to write has to have at least some element of the desire to be read.

Because I believe this I think that knowing how to go about testing the waters with your writing, how to get someone to read it attentively (even if they do not like it), is a large part of finding ways to get your work finished. So, in the final chapter I am going to look at things you might do next – after the writing is in one sense ofr another 'cooked', ready, done.

Chapter 8 Where to

A ll writers need readers. Until someone has read what you have written there is a sense in which the work is not finished.

What this chapter will look at is how to give yourself the best chances of success. Whether or not you feel comfortable about it, your writing needs to be read. I have assumed throughout that, at least at some levels of consciousness, you want it to be read. If you were happy just scrawling away in a private journal you would probably not have bought this book and pursued it this far.

There are many different sorts of creative writing, and so many different sorts of publishing: books, magazines, radio, TV, films, plays, competitions, websites – all of them highly competitive markets. Your writing is not going to be quite like anyone else's, so a book like this cannot give you specific advice. But there are some things that apply to everyone.

The first thing is to be honest. You have written something that you think is good enough to be allowed out into the world. You may, and probably should, feel a bit tentative about it, but another part of you knows that you cannot tell quite what you have achieved until you get some response. You want a reader. You probably want lots of readers actually, but for now let us just think about the first one. Obviously, you think, the very people to show your writing to are those closest to you – your family and friends.

Dispassionate critics

The problem is that friends and family are usually the worst possible readers. It is useful to understand why this is the case.

In the first place you have mixed feelings. You have put a lot of work, and probably a good deal of yourself into the writing – you really want them to like it. At the same time, you are very aware that it is not perfect, so if your reader says it is *wonderful* you will not be

next?

able to trust them. Moreover you are asking them for a good deal of time and attention – just asking for this can be quite difficult

Now try and see it from the reader's point of view. They know it is important to you, and (assuming you have chosen sensibly) they want to affirm, encourage and support you. At the same time they really want the writing to be good and they may well be slightly jealous of you because you have achieved a real ambition. They may well not know very much about writing and reading, and they may not have a clear useful vocabulary to discuss their feelings. Moreover they too are aware that you are asking for a good deal of their time and attention, which they both want to offer and resent giving.

You can begin to see why the whole thing is fraught with emotional problems.

Finding the right critic

In short, it is worth thinking quite carefully about who will be the first person that you ask. If you know other writers, it is easy; they will have some inkling of what it is that you need from them. If you don't, try and think of someone who is used to giving supportive criticism – for example schoolteachers, the parents of happy teenagers, health visitors. You also need someone who reads a lot and enjoys reading. Above all try and avoid anyone who might, rightly or wrongly, for any reason and at any level, feel that the writing is about them. They will be aggressive or defensive or both – and it is not fair on either of you.

All my experience tells me that most people are keen to read what their friends have been writing, but are uncertain how to respond to it. Don't thrust it into their hands while they are busy and say, 'What do you think of this?' and then hover about while they look at it. Try this approach:

❖ Ask your selected reader if s/he would like to see it

❖ If so wait a few days and then give them a tidy easy-to-read manuscript, in an envelope

❖ Suggest a time-frame ('Perhaps we could talk about it at the end of the month?')

❖ Tell them what you want from them – something they can respond to: 'I'm worried that the plot isn't really credible/ I've found the conversations really difficult – do you think they read naturally?/Do you find the protagonist sympathetic?'

Make sure the questions are real ones – ones you want to hear an honest answer to.

The idea behind asking specific questions is that it gives your readers a starting place. They know what you want, and they may be tempted to pay you lip service as they want to encourage you. Make it clear to them that you would like an honest reaction to your work. That gives them the opportunity to think of other more interesting things to say or point out, as well. Unless this reader is a professional reader (and even then be careful) never ask them if they think it is publishable. It is not a question on which they can have any useful opinion.

Whatever their response, listen carefully, respond to their questions but do not argue with them. Always thank them for reading it. One of the things you need to do as a writer is train some readers. They need affirmation in this tricky role nearly as much as you do. Remember: you do not have to agree with anything they say, or change your writing to meet their wishes. But having asked them to read it you owe them gratitude and serious attention to their comments.

Some writers do build up a relationship of mutual support with what I will call their domestic readers; William and Dorothy Wordsworth would be a good example. But unless the friend is also a writer, or knows a great deal about writing, most writers come to feel that they need readers who are less personally involved.

As well as needing readers, I think that most (though not all) writers need other people to talk *about* writing with. Writing is an isolated task, but communication is a social task: you need to balance the two.

Writing groups

The most straightforward way to get both direct readers and writer-talk is to join a writing group. Here the implicit contract is absolutely clear: I will read and respond to your writing because you will read and respond to mine; and we will do this as equals. There is no better training for a writer than a good and sympathetic writing group. Unfortunately not all writing groups are either good or sympathetic. You may have to look around to find the sort of group you want: ask around your friends for recommendations, or ask in your local library, adult education centre or look in your local newspaper. Be patient – give any group a couple of sessions of your time at least. But if you are certain the group is not for you leave before you waste too much of your and the other members' time.

If you cannot find a satisfactory local group it is worth trying a *reading* group (also called book groups). These have recently become incredibly popular and there should be one in your local area. If not, and the idea appeals to you, you could look into starting one up. Here you will get talk about writing – probably better (or at least more commercial) writing than in most writing groups; you will find less egotism and competitiveness; and you will meet people interested in writing – potential friends, colleagues and indeed readers.

Creative writing courses

The other place to find support, collegiality and an audience, as well as further developing your writing skills, is a creative writing course. Such courses are immensely popular, are available almost everywhere and can be very good indeed. Courses range from local evening courses to PhDs in creative writing (now on offer at various universities) – so you should be able to find something that will suit you.

Apart from university degrees in creative writing, courses tend to come in two forms: short intensive courses (usually residential) like those offered by The Arvon Foundation; and longer-term one-evening-a-week type courses which tend to be more local. Think clearly about what you need and want before committing yourself, although obviously there is no reason why you cannot do both. There are also one-off learning events – day workshops, classes, lectures and so on. Hearing professional writers, especially those whose work you feel attuned to, reading aloud and discussing their work is also a valuable 'course' or development opportunity, which you can (and should) explore: again, ask your library how you can get onto the local mailing lists for these events.

For people who live where there is no access to evening courses, or who for personal reasons cannot commit themselves to a regular event, or are the sort of people who prefer this, there are also distance-learning courses. For writing in particular there is a strong case for distance-learning: you will get the undivided attention of a qualified teacher/writer, so to a greater extent you can study what you want; the whole course (including the teaching) will be in the medium you are trying to study – *writing* itself; and you will be able to match the work on the assignments or units to your own writing schedule. The Open College of the Arts, for instance, runs correspondence writing courses at all levels, which are properly accredited.

You may have heard of MA courses in creative writing. Many universities run these (and some run them with a distance-learning strand as well as a residential one). These are for writers who have already established themselves in one way or another and give you opportunities both to work with a one-to-one supervisor and to form a group of colleagues and peers through the workshop sessions. I am mentioning these now because most of them will expect applicants to have attended courses or to have undertaken training of some sort before they apply. So quite apart from the direct benefits to your writing, it is worth finding out what sort of learning process suits you and using everything available.

Be patient — give any group a couple of sessions of your time at least

Getting your writing read

There are other important ways of getting your writing read and responded to:

❖ Competitions

In websites, writers' magazines, local libraries and by word of mouth you can discover a remarkable range of writing competitions – with categories ranging from single poems to whole novels. Many of the organizers will also provide (usually for an extra fee) critical feedback on your submission. Quite apart from any other benefits, entering for these competitions will oblige you to prepare, finish and present your work properly, and help discipline you to fully finish pieces of work that deserve that treatment. In the long run it is usually through competitions that writers build up a track record and any 'credits' – even being short listed for the major competitions – will improve your chances of interesting an agent or publisher in your work. For poets this is particularly crucial. If you are serious about becoming a published writer you should be entering all the competitions you can find out about. Be sure you read the submission rules carefully (for example, the minimum and maximum word lengths) and never expect anyone to bend them for you.

Many competitions have an enormous number of entries. They have to whittle these down to a short list of perhaps six. From these probably rather diverse works they have to choose a winner and other prizewinners. Inevitably an element of luck is going to come into play. When you enter a competition you need to accept that if you win, or are short-listed, then your work was good. Be pleased. However if you do not make the cut, it does not mean that your work is bad. You need to enter with hope, but not feel judged negatively whatever the outcome.

❖ **Professional readers**

Once upon a time publishers read (and bought) works from writers they had never heard of. More importantly they also prided themselves on 'talent spotting'; on finding new writers and working with them to bring their first (and subsequent) works to completion. On the whole publishing houses did not even expect to make a profit on first books, but hoped to woo and charm the writer into bringing the second and third book back, until their investment had paid off.

It is not like that now. Publishers expect books to be delivered to them more or less ready for printing. Usually they expect an agent to have done the initial work and only offer them books that are likely to appeal to them. Because they can get all the books they want this way they are increasingly unlikely to consider seriously any writers without an agent. Obviously this shift has sharply increased the power of agents. It has also increased their workload and they too have begun to follow the publishers down the path that says, 'We do not need to work with "nearly-there" writers; we only want to represent people whose writing is ready to sell'. So do not expect a publisher or an agent to be interested in your work until you feel that it is fully developed and commercially viable. At the same time you may well reach the point of feeling that although your writing is growing and getting stronger all the time, and your ideas have congealed into something that feels like a book, you really need some highly professional feedback and advice. This need has been recognised commercially by a new breed of professional readers or consultants who will – for a fee – work with you on your book. This cannot, and should not, be cheap so do not go to a consultancy until your writing is *as good as you can make it on your own*. (You do not need to spend your money being told something that you could have worked out for yourself.) However many writers will attest to the value of good professional consultants and it is certainly useful to know that they are there should you have need of them.

N.B.: Consultants are not vanity presses. Vanity presses offer to publish your manuscript at your expense. Professional readers offer to help you improve your manuscript so that a commercial publisher may wish to purchase it.

❖ **Agents**

A good agent is perhaps the best writing ally you can possibly have; a bad agent is a waste of your energy. Literary agents act

Entering competitions will oblige you to prepare, finish and present your work properly

as the interface between a writer and the professional world – selling your work through their knowledge of the various markets. Agents do not charge a fee but take a percentage commission, so they will work with writers whom they believe will make them enough money. They want professionals. So if you approach an agent, make sure your work looks professional – this includes finding out precisely what a particular agent wants to see (usually quite a short sample) and not sending anything else. You can always phone or email to check. Rremember, rejection by an agent is not a comment on your writing, but a quick assessment of your probable profit to that agent. The sort of reading and support they can give you is related to that aspect of your work. As you grow as a writer you will need all the friends and colleagues you can get. Treat them nicely.

❖ **Publishers**

Eventually, you may decide to send your writing somewhere for potential publication. Again, be very careful that your particular work is in line with what they actually publish – there is no point in sending a romantic short story to a magazine that is for steam-train enthusiasts, for example. When you think you are ready to publish you can find very good advice from books, writers' magazines and websites. There are also lists of publishers with comments on the sort of work they take and what their submissions policy is. Read this carefully. Go to a bookshop or library and see whether you like the way their books look. Above all, don't get disheartened: remember lots of writers who are now internationally famous had real problems at first. *Watership Down* received over 50 rejections before Richard Adams got it published. Try to deal with rejections in a business-like way; read and think about any comments you may get and then send out the next batch of sample text to the next publishing houses on your list.

Presenting your manuscript

One fundamental way of treating people 'nicely' is to treat them, and particularly their time, with respect. Among other things, this means that when you want them to read or listen to your work, they deserve to have it decently presented. Of course you can show people you know well, especially if they are colleagues, rough drafts of something for discussion – but you need to be straightforward about it. Don't pretend something is finished if it isn't; and equally don't ask them to read sloppy, uncorrected, badly presented, scrawled material. Apart from anything else if you make it a personal rule only to show people properly finished text, it will give you a good practice in the important art of giving your work the best chance it can get.

Here is a list of presentation points that professionals expect from almost any manuscript. Where it is relevant I have tried to explain why it matters.

❖ **Standard spelling**. Although a primary school teacher is trying to encourage fluency and creativity in their pupils' writing and may often feel that too many corrected spellings will not help, readers are trying to get pleasure. Inaccurate spelling will distract them from the reading experience and this will diminish their pleasure (unless of course the unusual spelling is part of the designed pleasure). Use a spell check. And check the spell check, which can only do what it can do – it cannot, for example, as I have mentioned before, distinguish between 'there', 'their' and 'they're' or between 'of the' and 'oft he', even if one of those makes no sense at all in a particular context.

❖ **Readable text.** This means a sensible font – Times New Roman or Arial are the usual professional fonts. Reading more than about a page in comic sans or COMPACTA is wearisome in a reasonable size (12 or 10 point depending on the font). You also want a wide margin and a reasonable space between the lines (1.5 or double space). Oddly enough it is better not to justify your text (where it all lines up on the right-hand side of the page as well as the left). You might think that it looks more professional that way, but actually it is much harder to see minor mistakes and be certain about gaps between the words.

❖ **Effective punctuation.** Unlike spelling punctuation is not (usually) a matter of correct or incorrect. It is part of the writing itself – it matters in the same way that a sensible adjective matters. It instructs the reader, however subliminally, on how to read the writing. The one place where punctuation is purely conventional is in conversation. This is to help the reader know who is speaking and which parts of the sentence are also parts of the conversation. Some contemporary writers have started using different conventions, but even they will follow their own rule throughout. The important things are consistency and clarity.

❖ **Sensible paper.** Keep it simple – A4, white, neither absurdly flimsy (it tears, crumples and you can't write comments on it, or erase them afterwards) nor massively thick (it makes the manuscript unwieldy and heavy). Print on one side of the paper only and don't put it into a binder, or staple anything. Number the pages.

I can hear a bossy tone creeping up on me. I sort of apologize. But I also sort of don't. In my work I have to read a lot of manuscripts, and believe me it makes an enormous difference if the manuscript is pleasant and convenient – well typed and well laid out – to work with. I feel more warmly towards the writer as a fellow professional. I feel they have treated me courteously and respectfully, and I find myself responding in kind. Your writing deserves to be given the best chance you can give it to make friends out there in what is not always a kindly and generous world.

There are a number of books that go into these particulars in more detail. You will find some recommendations in the next section. And finally, remember that when you set out on your writing journey you are not just trying an experiment in self-expression, you are also becoming a creator and guardian of a living language, in its written form.

If you have any doubts about any of these points, or other points of presentation or grammar, consult one of them. Even if you think you are 'good at' grammar and language use, add a couple of books to your writing reference library. They are interesting, and can be fun, as well as useful. In *The Creative Writing Coursebook*. ed. Julia Bell and Paul Magrs (Macmillan, 2003), for example, there is a chapter by Penny Rendall on how to present your manuscript in terms of punctuation, grammar and so on, to publishers, editors and agents. She does not just say what, she explains why and I think it is the best short piece on the subject I have encountered.

It matters. Enjoy it, and good luck.

A note on grammar

It is very difficult to write about writing without using a certain number of technical terms. Here and there in this book, I have explained what I mean by particular expressions, but for those people who are a bit scared of grammar, or who were educated without being taught the official terms, I hope this very brief appendix will be helpful. I apologise for its brevity and stress that it is very much a quick reference guide to help with your appreciation of this book. In the bibliography I have suggested books that will explain grammar much better than I, and advise you further.

Verbs are the words that describe what is happening in a sentence. When I was a child it was called a 'doing word'. More than other English words verbs are 'inflected' – they change their form according to what is going on. For example:

- ❖ Who or what is doing the action: To be, I am, you are, she is. To run, I run, he runs, they run.
- ❖ When the action is taking place, this is called *tense*: I am running, I run, I was running, I ran, I will run (and there are lots more, for example, I will have run).
- ❖ Whether the action was done to someone or by someone: I bit him (this is called the *active voice*); I was bitten by him (*passive voice*).

Verbs are also described as *strong* or *weak*. A strong verb is one that directly describes the action; a weak one is one that requires propping up with more information. 'She tried very hard to solve the problem' is weaker (in grammatical terms) than 'she wrestled with the problem,' or 'the problem demanded her attention'.

Nouns are the words that represent things. *Concrete nouns* represent things you can see or touch – like table, cow, or machine. *Abstract nouns* represent things that have no material reality – like freedom, happiness and love. *Proper nouns* are names, they belong to something uniquely – like Sara, Germany,

Bovril. You can normally spot them because they are spelled with an initial capital letter, but the grammatical test is that normally they do not need 'the' or 'a' (these two words are called the *definite* and the *indefinite article*): 'A Germany' does not make much sense. *Collective nouns* are words that hold a whole group of something within them – like herd (of cows), class (of pupils) or family (of people related to each other).

Adverbs explain or describe *verbs* further. They often, but not always, end in 'ly' – quickly, slowly, softly, but also 'fast', and in the sentence 'She tried very hard to solve the problem' 'hard' is an adverb because it describes the sort of trying she was doing.

Adjectives on the other hand explain or describe *nouns* – like hot, red or sophisticated. So in the sentence 'She tried to solve the hard problem' 'hard' is an adjective because it describes the sort of problem (a noun).

Pronouns are words that stand in place of a noun, so that you do not have to go on reusing it – like I, you or them.

Conjunctions are words that link two bits of sentence together – like and, or and but.

There are lots of other parts of speech too, so if you have a word that does not seem to fit into any of these categories, do not worry.

Word order is obviously important so that we can make sense of what we are reading. 'The man bit the dog' and 'the dog bit the man' do not mean the same thing even though they use exactly the same words. In English the normal order is that the noun *doing* the verb (called the *subject*) goes before the verb, and the noun it was done to (the *object*) goes after the verb, but it is possible to do some things in various ways and get various different effects.

Punctuation

Punctuation is a very ingenious set of little marks that only exist on the page – they do not exist in spoken language, where their job is carried on by human breathing patterns, facial expressions and intonations. The sole purpose of punctuation marks is to help readers understand what they are reading. Bad punctuation can make even the most beautiful writing simply incomprehensible.

The principal punctuations marks are:

- **.** the *full stop* (or *period*) marks the end of a sentence. A sentence is the basic structure of language that allows us to make sense. It is extremely hard to define much further than this, beyond saying that it is the place where a speaker takes a proper new in-breath. It is simply not true that a sentence has to have a subject and a verb: what it has to have, by whatever means the writer chooses, is a coherent idea.

- **,** the *comma*, which suggests a shorter, lighter pause in the middle of sentences and is also used to divide words in lists.

- **;** the *semi-colon* could be described as somewhere between a full stop and a comma. It should be used to split up two parallel phrases when you want to keep them in the same sentence. So, 'She went to the party; it was fun but she left early'.

- **:** the *colon* has rather gone out of fashion. Its original use was to mark impressive contrasts (where the semi-colon merely marked parallels) as in 'Man proposes: God disposes'. However, it has re-emerged in a special context – what Fowler describes as 'delivering the goods that have been invoiced in the preceding words' – to start a list after you have said what the list is going to contain, e.g. 'There were lots of animals: cows with their calves, pigs, noisy turkeys and a great many hens'.

- **?** the *question* or *interrogation mark* quite simply shows that what you have written is a question.

!   the *exclamation mark* is used when you wish to show the heightened emotion of a phrase which is not a real or natural sentence.

-     the *hyphen* is used to link two words together so that the sentence may be more easily understood. 'Bach wrote 200-odd cantatas' means something different from 'Bach wrote 200 odd cantatas'. Or to create new words by combining old ones.

( )   the *bracket* or *parenthesis* belongs round a piece of writing that is grammatically irrelevant to the sentence, but not irrelevant to the meaning.

—   the *dash* can be used in a variety of ways: as a version of the bracket, or nowadays, it is often used instead of a semi-colon.

''   *quotations marks* (they are usually single in UK English, rather than the double ones US English more commonly uses) show that someone is speaking, or that the writing is quoting another author.

'   the *apostrophe* is something of an oddity – it does not replace anything from the spoken language. Instead it emphasizes something we do not emphasize in speech – it indicates either a *possessive* (John's book = this book belongs to John) or an *elision* where some letters have been left out of words (*they're* for *they are* or *don't* for *do not*).

       a *new paragraph* is shown by a full stop followed by a (usually indented) new line, and indicates that the writer is now moving on to a new topic or subject.

You will quickly notice that although I have given you the name of each of these punctuation marks and a brief definition, I have not told you the conventions (and in some cases rules) for using them. This is because to cover the subject fully would be, and indeed has been, the task of a whole book. Unless you are very confident, you should use the names I have given you to look the various marks up in a proper grammar book – I suggest some in the bibliography.

Further reading and

Reference books

Most writers love books and tend to accumulate them. However when you start it is worth remembering that all the books listed in this section – or a very similar equivalent – will be available in the reference section of your public library. You do not need to buy them all in order to get started.

A dictionary. I use the compact edition of the full Oxford English Dictionary, with its magnifying glass. But this is not necessary. Any dictionary will do; one with some historical background to individual words is best.

A thesaurus. A 'thesaurus' is a dictionary of synonyms; so it groups together words that mean more or less the same thing. The most famous English thesaurus is: *Roget's Thesaurus of English Words and Phrases*. ed. George Davidson (Penguin, 2004.) An edition of it is also available free at **www.thesaurus.com**.

The Oxford Companion to English Literature. ed. Margaret Drabble (OUP, 2000)

A Dictionary of Modern Critical Terms. ed. Roger Fowler (Routledge & Kegan Paul)

The New Fowler's Modern English Usage (3rd Ed) by H. W. Fowler (OUP)

The Careful Writer by Theodore M. Bernstein

Merriam-Webster's Dictionary of English Usage by Merriam-Webster

other resources

Creative writing books

General

Writing Down the Bones: freeing the writer within by Naomi Goldberg (Shambhala Publications, 1988)

The Creative Writing Coursebook. ed. Julia Bell and Paul Magrs (Macmillan, 2003)

The Way to Write by John Fairfax and John Moat (Penguin, 1998)

Fiction

Aspects of the Novel by E.M.Forster (Penguin, 1927) Despite its age (and therefore some inevitable limitations), I think this is the most helpful book about novel writing that I know.

What If?: Exercises for fiction writers by Anne Bernays and Pamela Painter (HarperResource, 1991)

The Lonely Voice: A Study of the Short Story by Frank O'Connor (Harper Colophon, 1985

Poetry

Art and Craft of Poetry by Michael Bugeja (Writers Digest Books, 1994)

How to Write Poetry by Nancy Bogan (Macmillan, 1998)

www.poetry-portal.com   www.poetrymagic.co.uk

Children's

Writer's Handbook Guide to Writing for Children by Barry Turner (Macmillan, 2004)

www.writewords.org   www.signaleader.com/childrens-writers

Index